The
HANDBOOK OF PRACTICAL CUTTING
on the Centre Point System (1866)

Illustrated with nearly 350 Model Patterns or Diagrams

by Louis Devere

Revised and Enlarged Edition, edited by R. L. Shep

R. L. Shep
Lopez Island

Copyright © 1986 by R. L. Shep

This edition contains the original work of 1866 & 1868 plus additional notes, material and illustrations.

ISBN 0-914046-03-9

Library of Congress #86-90526

Printed in the United States of America

Published by:
   R. L. SHEP
   Box C-20
   Lopez Island,
   Washington 98261

INTRODUCTORY NOTES

This work first appeared in 1866, as noted by Edward Giles in his *History of the Art of Cutting in England*. Louis Devere had studied under G. Compaing, who published *L'Art du Tailleur* in Paris in 1820. In 1847, Devere took over the "Gentleman's Magazine", which was started in 1828 by John Browne Bell. Devere reintroduced diagrams into this publication (they had been dropped in 1840) as well as instructions for drafting and cutting out, so that it became a journal really devoted to tailoring, and became the oldest English fashion journal for tailors, continuing at least into the 1890's. Devere went on with Compaing's son Charles to publish *The Tailor's Guide* in London in 1856. That work consisted of a system of tailoring based on 17 measures for the ordinary structure (body), and had been refined from 24 measurements in the work of 1820. The system was further refined to 11 measurements in 1860, and finally to only 6 in this work of 1866.

We have used the third edition both because we have it complete and in good condition, and because it gives clearer drafting instructions. The first two editions are identical and were printed one soon after the other, and Devere says that this edition followed the first in less than three years. (Printings were referred to as "editions" at that time even when there were no changes in them from the original.) There are changes in this edition. It is here that they adopted the name "The Centre Point System", which Devere says is the center of gravity of the human body (of any shape) – with it, one finds the true balance of the pattern required for each person. It must be remembered that garments were tailored to order and to fit one person. Mass-produced garments really began to find their way into the market only after John Barran developed the band knife, in 1860, which cut 30 to 40 layers of cloth at one time. However, before that, sweat shops in Leeds were producing garments in an assembly line style, usually having tailors do the finishing touches (this was especially true for uniforms and middle class garments). Needless to say, these were not worn by gentlemen.

The other changes in this edition deal with clarifications in the drafting system for stout builds and clarification of the method of measuring. The plates remain the same with the exception of plate 21, which deals with uniforms. The original from the first edition has been included on the reverse of the plate in this edition for comparison.

Originally, this book measured 5½ inches high by 7½ inches long, which meant that the illustrations were very small. We have had the pages enlarged so that the cutting diagrams can be seen more clearly, and have placed the plates where they should fall in the text rather than in a separate volume. We have also combined the four tables of contents, rather than having them at the beginning of each section, and have dropped Devere's preface, which dealt mostly with the fact that he hoped to bring out a new work entitled *The Complete Manual of Cutting*. Part One of that work was published in 1875. Giles does not mention any further parts being published; therefore, we can presume they were not, as Devere must have been elderly at the time. It might also be worth noting at this point that a "cheap edition" of *The Handbook of Practical Cutting* with only 24 plates came out at a later date, which bears out our contention that it was useful beyond the exact period it was written in. Giles says that the centre point, or fixed point, system was both unique and original, and not used in this manner by any other author. In talking about the tailoring of trousers, he says he does not know who first introduced the front line for a basis to produce them, but that Devere's method was well known and a good example of this system. He also says that Devere's attention to minute details of tailoring and of fit makes the centre point system rank among the best in tailoring literature.

By noting details of fashions of the time, this work can be used to make garments from about 1850 right up through the 1870's. Allowances are made in the diagrams so that they can be adjusted to changing fashions.

As usual, it is much easier to find information about the women's fashions of the period than it is of the men's. This was, of course, the age of the crinoline, at least until the mid-60's (when the bustle started to be worn). The few women's garments dealt with in this work are paletots, which were a type of mantle (also often called a visite or pardessus); riding habits, including a long train; and a pattern for "Ladies' Riding Trowsers". Devere claims that this is the first time a diagram for them has been printed. Women did not ride astride, but often wore trousers under a 'break-away skirt' in case they were thrown, although this is not even alluded to at such an early date.

Let's look briefly at gentlemen's dress, using the 1850's as a base and noting the changes as they occur later on. Anne Buck points out, very rightly, that men's fashions are more influenced by the occasion on which they are worn than women's. And Janet Burgess reminds us that we always have to pay attention to who the person was to determine what he would have worn at any particular time. Edward Giles says that the general character of men's costume did not undergo any change during the entire Victorian era, but that there were continual modifications and variations in styles and details. He says that the greatest change was amongst the labouring and working classes – the linen smock-frock being replaced by the shooting coat, and that fustian (a dark, heavy cotton twill) and corduroy trousers were relegated to the lower orders, such as barrow boys, peddlers and day labourers, and replaced by tweed trousers. For gentlemen, it was a matter of coats becoming longer or shorter, sleeves and trousers wider or narrower, etc. Also, the functions of certain garments changed: e.g., breeches, which were worn generally at one time, later were worn by gentlemen for hunting and by servants for livery. Tailcoats were also generally worn at one time, but by Victorian times they were worn on formal occasions only.

1850's: Coats – frock coats (somewhat shaped) were universally worn daytime, often with a velvet collar.
- morning coats (cut with a sloping front) were for informal day wear.
- sack or lounge jackets appeared (single and double breasted), to be worn, very informally, in the country or at the seaside.
- tailcoats (cut straight across in front at the waist) were for formal wear and of dark, but not necessarily black, fabric.

Trousers were narrow and of a different color than the coat, with a buttoned fly front, no pleats, and worn with embroidered braces or suspenders.

Waistcoats were very fancy (embroidered or brocade), single and double breasted, slightly cut away at the front. Single-breasted white only were worn for formal wear.

Cravats were the loose scarf type, black in the evening, and white for very formal wear.

Shirts were white with a fairly high or winged collar; they often had ruffles in the front, but were pleated for formal wear.

Shoes were square toed and laced or with elastic sides; also short boots were worn; and gaiters were worn with both.

Overcoats were of many types: Raglans (1857), Chesterfields, Inverness capes, mantles, capes, and short jackets with big buttons.

Top hats and gloves were worn in town, and straw sailor hats more informally.

'Ditto suits' – 3-piece suits all the same fabric (often loud stripes) appeared, extremely informal (seaside wear).

Shooting jackets were short frock coats.

1860's: Frock coats were less shaped at the waist and sleeves were wide at top, narrowing to the cuff (especially during the first half of the period).

Sack/lounge coats came into general daytime use, morning coats worn for formal daytime, and tails (black only) for formal evening wear. Coats were buttoned higher (sometimes only the top button).

Trousers were 'peg top' – wide at the top and narrow at the bottom – in the early years and then started to narrow again; they often had braid or a stripe down the side. Knickerbockers were for sport and country wear.

Waistcoats were shorter and cut straight across at the waist, and no longer fancy. They matched either the coat or the trousers.

Cravats narrowed, worn in a bow or knot in daytime, and shirt collars rolled lower.

Shoes and boots buttoned, the toes were longer and more rounded; gaiters were worn less often.

Top hats shortened to a six-inch crown in the mid-60's, and the bowler hat came in; gloves were worn and walking sticks were indispensable.

Disposable collars appeared and 'Ditto' suits were more common.

1870's: Frock coats had straight sleeves, cuffed with two buttons.

Trousers were generally narrower, and often plaid.

Waistcoats were a bit longer, but still cut straight across the waist.

Sack/lounge suits and 'Ditto' suits were in widespread use.

Shoes still buttoned but were more pointed.

Hats with dented crown and curved brim (later called a "trilby" from the du Maurier novel) were worn in addition to those noted before.

Some patterned shirts were worn during the day (but not many) and white shirts lost their ruffles, but were still pleated for evening.

N.B. In Devere, the Morning jacket is the Morning Coat; Dress coat is the Tailcoat; Oxonian coats are Sack or Lounge Jackets. Pea Jackets and Reefers are middle class and farmers' outerwear.

Janet Burgess, in her notes on Civil War costume, paints a more somber picture for the 1860's in the United States, except that waistcoats seem to have remained fancy for a longer period. The colors in general for jackets, coats and trousers were very dark, and many men wore shawls.

RESEARCH: We have reproduced a few fashion plates to give you some idea of what to look for. These are drawings, so they represent the ideal of male beauty as well as the ideal of fashion, showing future trends. Pick up a current magazine that shows a lot of men's fashions and ask yourself, especially if the illustrations are sketches rather than photographs, "Who do I know who looks and dresses like that?"

Drawings A and B are both from a late-1849 issue of *"L'Elegant"*, a French fashion magazine. They are in fact showing many of the trends for the 1850's. The hats are tall (with the exception of the riding cap, of course), the waists are quite suppressed (we know that men wore corsets when necessary to achieve a fashionable figure), the waistcoats are slightly cut-away in front and are fancy, the collars are high, the cravats are still quite large, and the shoes are very square. In drawing A, the man on the left is probably wearing a tailcoat (it is hard to see) which is cut straight at the waist; the man in the middle is obviously wearing a frock coat; and the really interesting thing about the man on the right is the very large buttons on his jacket. The collars and cravats differ for each person. The styles in drawing B are far less formal: the man on the left is wearing a shooting jacket; the one in the middle is probably wearing a very early lounge jacket (the upper closure is very informal); and the man on the right is wearing a morning coat. Drawing B certainly points up the fact that none of the three pieces match and that the waistcoats were very fancy.

Drawing C is from the same magazine twenty years later (1869) and shows how much more relaxed the styles had become. These men are in fashionable day wear for the time. The crowns of the hats are definitely shorter; they are both wearing lounge jackets, one single and one double breasted (or we could be seeing a very short frock coat, which I do not believe). Note the stripe on the trousers of the man on the left and the fact that there is a lot of pattern in both the trousers; the jackets are closing higher and the waistcoats have become less important; collars are rolled much lower; both men are wearing gloves and carrying walking sticks. It must be remembered that if they were showing more formal wear, the men would be wearing tailcoats in the evening and morning coats in the daytime; and if they were showing a country or seaside scene, we would see 'ditto' suits, straw hats, etc.

SOURCES (those marked * have men's sections):

Boucher, Francois. *20,000 Years of Fashion.* NY. (1966.)

Brooke, Iris. *English Costume of the Nineteenth Century.* NY. 1977.

Brooke, Iris & Laver, James. *English Costume from the 14-19th Centuries.* NY. 1937.

*Buck, Anne. *Victorian Costume.* UK. 1984.

*Burgess, Janet. *Clothing Guidelines for the Civil War Era.* Iowa. 1985.

Collard, Eileen. *Cut of Women's Dress 19th Century: VICTORIAN GOTHIC 1840-66.* Canada. 1978.

Davenport, Millia. *Book of Costume.* NY. 1948. (good illustrations)

*Giles, Edward. *The History of the Art of Cutting in England.* London. 1896.

*Lansdell, Avril. *Fashion a la Carte 1860-1900.* UK. 1985.

Laver, James. *Costume.* NY. 1963.

Laver, James. *Taste & Fashion from the French Revolution to the Present.* London. 1948.

*Payne, Blanche. *History of Costume.* NY. 1965.

*Winter, Janet & Schultz, Carolyn. *Victorian Costuming: 1840-1865.* Oakland. 1980.

Drawing C

Drawing A

Drawing B

CONTENTS OF PART 1.

CONTENTS OF PART 2.

CONTENTS OF PART 3.

CONTENTS OF PART 4.

THE

HANDBOOK OF PRACTICAL CUTTING,

ON THE CENTRE POINT SYSTEM,

BY

LOUIS DEVERE,

Editor of "The Gentleman's Magazine of Fashion," "The Cutters' Monthly Journal," and "Devere's Report of Fashion," Author of "The Tailors' Guide," "The Complete Manual of Cutting, &c.

CONTAINING NEARLY 350 MODEL PATTERNS OR DIAGRAMS.

London :

SIMPKIN, MARSHALL, & Co., STATIONERS' COURT,

And all Booksellers in town and country.

** ENTERED AT STATIONERS' HALL.

DEVERE'S

CENTRE POINT SYSTEM OF CUTTING.

PART THE FIRST.

INTRODUCTION.

(Plate 1.)

In commencing the practical study of the Art of Cutting, the young student must first procure the requisite instruments, which are indeed those generally used in the trade; namely, the Common Inch Tape, the Common Inch Ruler, the Square, and the Graduated Measures.

The Common Inch Tape is used for taking the measures of the client.

Fig. 1 shows the Common Inch Ruler, which is useful for drafting patterns for $18\frac{3}{4}$ breast measure: it is also used for drawing all long straight lines.

Fig. 2 is a Square, which is used in drafting, for drawing lines square with the construction lines. We have adopted this form, because it

(Plate 1.)

is always accurate, while we have found that the folding squares become incorrect, after the joint has worn a little in use.

The Graduated Measures, are a series of measures, which are successively graduated larger and smaller than the common inch measure, and are used to draft patterns for larger or smaller sizes than the $18\frac{3}{4}$ breast. The "CENTRE POINT SYSTEM" can be worked correctly by DEVERE'S GRADUATED MEASURES only. All other measures are drafted on a wrong base, and would make the patterns too large. The reason is this.—That the 18-inch base used by the early graduated measures makers was not founded upon a correct proportional standard. It was taken, because the introducers had not sufficient mathematical

B

(Plate 1.)

talent to form a scale with the proper divisions. *Devere's* Graduated Measures, may be had on paper, on tapes, or on wooden rulers. Figs. 3 and 4 show one side of the Graduated Measures on wooden rulers, the end of each ruler being broad enough to act as a square.

In addition to these our student will have to provide himself with some large sheets of white or brown paper, on which to draft the patterns. For drawing the lines, he may use black lead pencil or chalk: black lead pencil will suit the white paper, chalk the brown. We prefer brown paper, and the most useful and convenient for drafting, is made in sheets 46 inches × 36 inches, called " Casing " by the paper Merchants.

HOW TO
DRAFT PATTERNS THE FULL SIZE.

(Plates 1, 2.)

The first thing to learn is, how to draft a pattern the natural size by the common inch tape, and for this we proceed as follows:—

Suppose we wish to draft the forepart, fig. 1,

(Plates 1, 2.)

in *plate 2*, we have to perform the four successive operations, shown by figs. 5 to 8, of *plate 1.*

Fig. 5. We draw first a straight line, called the *Line of Construction*, and make a mark at the top (at 0). Starting from this point, we then mark, with the common inch measure, at all the distances indicated on the construction line of fig. 1, plate 2 ; namely, at 4 for the slope of shoulder seam ; at $7\frac{1}{2}$ for the top of side point ; at 10 for the bottom of scye ; at $18\frac{1}{8}$ for the hollow of waist ; and at $19\frac{3}{4}$ for the bottom of side and of front edge.

Fig. 6. This being done, we take the Square, and with it draw lines square across from all these points.

Fig. 7. With the common inch measure, we mark on each of the square lines, the *widths* indicated on fig. 1, *plate 2* ; which are as follows :— $9\frac{1}{2}$ for the shoulder point ; $14\frac{1}{4}$ for the neck point ; $1\frac{1}{2}$ for the side point, and $6\frac{3}{4}$ for the front of scye ; $4\frac{3}{4}$ for the bottom of scye, and $15\frac{3}{4}$ for the hollow of the hip ; $4\frac{3}{4}$ for the front edge ; $4\frac{3}{4}$ for the hollow of the hip ; $1\frac{3}{8}$ for the bottom of side seam, and $14\frac{1}{4}$ for the

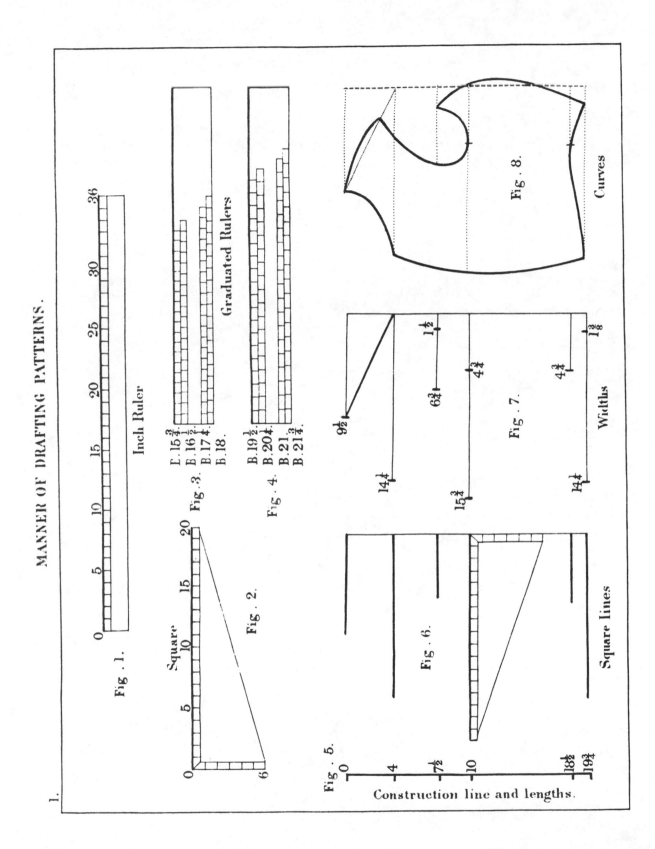

MANNER OF DRAFTING PATTERNS.

(Plates 1, 2.)

bottom of front edge. We then draw the sloping line of shoulder seam, from $9\frac{1}{2}$ to 4.

Fig. 8. The pattern is completed by drawing all the curves by the hand. We do not at all recommend the practice of sweeping or casting the curves, which some have proposed for beginners. It is a slow laborious process, and produces a stiff unartistic style of pattern. It is of the greatest importance that the young Cutter should be able to draw the curves well, and to attain this end we shall return to this subject of the curves, in describing *plate 3*, and shall give a very simple and easy way of learning how to form them.

We may observe that the back, fig. 2, and sleeve, fig. 3, in *plate 2*, are to be drafted as we have described for the forepart.

HOW TO
VARY THE SIZE OF A PATTERN.

(Plate 2.)

The pattern which we have just drafted by the common inch tape, is for a man measuring $18\frac{3}{4}$ breast, and *the common inch will always*

(Plate 2.)

produce our patterns for this size only. If we require patterns for larger or smaller breast measures, we obtain them without any trouble or calculation, by simply using a larger or smaller graduated measure, to mark the various points of the pattern, in place of the common inch tape. If when drafting our pattern, we had used a small graduated measure, say the one marked B. $15\frac{3}{4}$, we should have a pattern for a $15\frac{3}{4}$ breast, fig. 4. If we had used a larger measure, say B. 21 breast, fig. 21, we should have a pattern for a 21 breast, all the parts of the pattern being decreased or increased in exact proportion.

This is the simplest possible method of increasing or decreasing the size of a pattern, and is the only accurate one that was ever invented. Some cutters of the old school indeed, have objected to the use of the graduated measures, as something derogatory to their dignity, but they should consider that the graduated measures, or scales, are used by all artists, architects, and surveyors, and are indeed indispensible adjuncts to every kind of art.

THE
PROPORTIONATE PATTERN.
(Plate 3.)

The back and forepart which we have just drafted from, figs. 1 and 2, plate 2, are really the MODEL TYPE OR PROPORTIONATE PATTERN, and this is of so much importance, that we have given it again on a much larger scale, fig. 1, plate 3, so that it may be more easily studied. The back and forepart are placed side by side in two squares, each square being exactly the width of the piece which is contained in it. The back stretch and side point being also placed on the same level, we see at a glance the difference that exists in length between the back and forepart, a thing which is of far more importance, than is generally imagined.

The *Well Proportioned Man* has his body of medium length, neither long nor short: he is neither thin nor stout at waist: his attitude is upright, neither stooping nor standing extra erect: his shoulders are of moderate size, and are neither high nor low.

In our system, the proportionate pattern, being

(Plate 3.)

the medium between all other patterns, serves as a base or starting point, from which we may make all the variations and deviations required by the different structures : it is therefore of great importance, and all the figures of this pattern should be committed to memory, so that the student may be able at any time to draft the model type without the aid of the diagram, and may also be able when he sees any diagram, to know at a glance how and where it deviates from the true proportionate standard.

This proportionate pattern is also valuable, in cases where we may not be able to take the measures of the client, which may happen from various causes in cases of emergency, and a coat made from this pattern, while it would of course fit the best on a person who was proportionate, would still not look amiss, on a man who was slightly longer or shorter bodied, stooping or extra erect, thinner or stouter at waist. The ready-made houses in fact, draft *all* their coats from the proportionate pattern, and have found this plan tolerably successful.

HOW TO VARY THE SIZE.

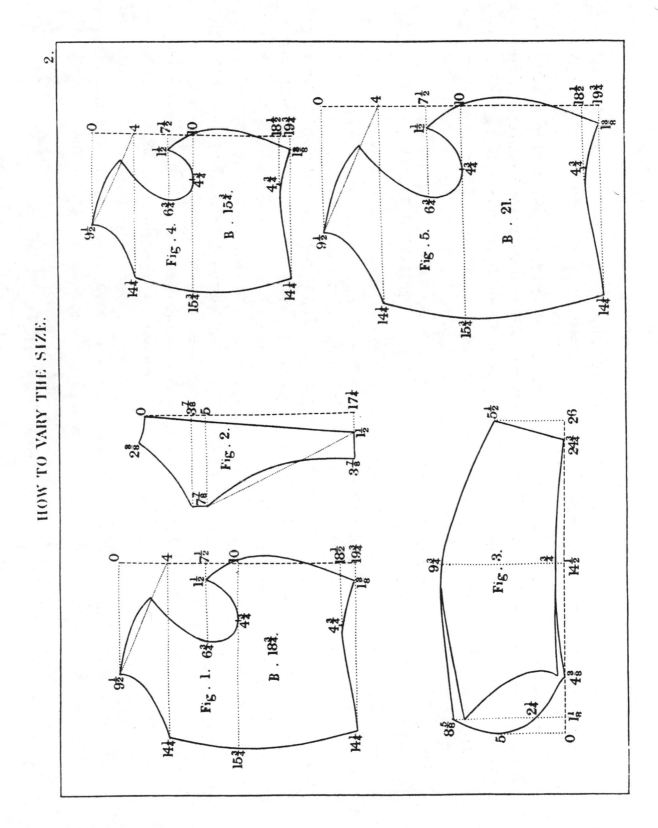

(Plate 3.)

We will now examine in detail the dimensions of this pattern, and will call attention to those points which vary, for disproportionate structures.

The square which contains the forepart has a width of 15¾, and that for the back is half that width, 7⅞. This 7⅞ we may observe, does not indicate the real width of back stretch, because the middle of back slopes in from the construction line, so that the back stretch is really only about 7½ wide.

BACK.

The *difference* between the lengths of back and forepart is 2½ inches. It may be more or less, if the structure is extra erect or stooping.

The length of back is 17¼, but it may be more or less if the man is long or short bodied.

The depth of the bottom of back scye is ¾ more than one fourth the length of back. The top of back scye is 1⅛ above this.

The widths of back neck and of back at waist, are each 2⅜, but this 2⅜ may at times vary according to Fashion.

(Plate 3.)

FOREPART.

The first point we have to notice is, that the full length is 19¾; that is, equal to the length of back 17¼, plus the distance of the top of back from the corner of the square, (2½).

The slope of the slanting line which rules the shoulder seam, is 4. It may be more or less if the shoulder is high or low, large or small.

The height of side point is 7½. It is always on a level with the bottom of back stretch.

The bottom of scye is at 10, or 2½ below the side point. This depth may be more or less if the shoulder is high or low, large or small.

The hollow of waist is at 18½, or 1¼ less than the length of forepart. This hollowing of waist is *always* 1¼ graduated inches.

The shoulder point is at 9½, and this is a fixed point in almost every case, and is but rarely subject to variation.

The neck point is at 14¼, or 1½ in from the the outside of square.

The taking in of side point is 1½. This is also a fixed point.

(Plate 3.)

The front of scye is at $6\frac{3}{4}$, but may be more or less if the shoulders are forward or backward.

The bottom of scye is $4\frac{3}{4}$, for all structures.

The full width across the chest is $15\frac{3}{4}$. This width may be a little more or less, if the chest is round or flat.

The hollow of hips or *Centre Point* is at $4\frac{3}{4}$, and the middle of waist is at $6\frac{1}{2}$. These are fixed and invariable points in all cases.

The taking in of the bottom of side seam is $1\frac{3}{8}$. This may be less if the waist is stout, and may even go outside the square.

The front of waist is at $14\frac{1}{4}$, or $1\frac{1}{2}$ less than the width of square. If the waist is stout, this point may be nearer the outside of square, and may even be carried beyond it.

HOW TO DRAW THE CURVES.

The curves of this pattern still require examination, and in order to explain them as clearly as possible, we have placed straight dotted lines between all the principal points, and have marked *in graduated inches*, the distances that the

(Plate 3.)

curves should be hollowed in or sprung out from these lines, as we will now describe, commencing with

THE BACK.

For the back neck; draw a line square from 0, and at $2\frac{3}{8}$, rise up $\frac{1}{4}$ a graduated inch for the curve of neck seam.

For the shoulder seam; draw a straight line from the neck to the top of back scye, and hollow in $\frac{3}{8}$ from this line. This seam may have more or less hollow according to Fashion.

For the side seam. Draw an oblique line from the bottom of back stretch, to the middle of back at waist. Then starting from the top, mark at 4 along the line, for the place where the curve has the greatest hollow: at this place, mark inside the line, $\frac{3}{8}$ of a graduated inch for the hollowing in of side seam. This $\frac{3}{4}$ may be more or less according to Fashion: draw the seam in a regular curve.

THE FOREPART.

For the shoulder seam. Mark first the length, to correspond with the shoulder seam of back.

THE STANDARD PATTERN, HOW TO DRAW THE CURVES.

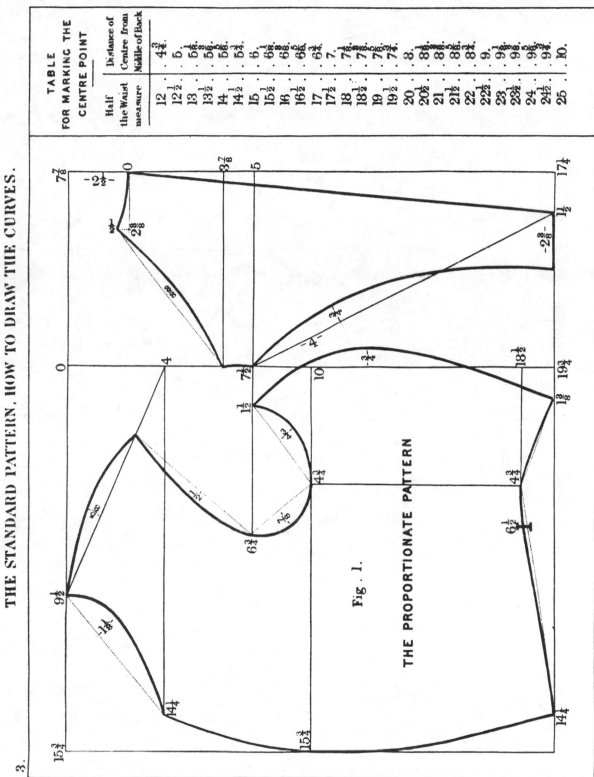

Fig. 1.

THE PROPORTIONATE PATTERN

HOW TO DRAW THE CURVES.

(Plates 3.)

In the centre of the seam, mark outside for the curve, $\frac{1}{4}$ of *a graduated inch more* than the hollowing of the shoulder seam at back : if the back is hollowed $\frac{3}{8}$, the forepart must be rounded $\frac{5}{8}$; if the back is hollowed $\frac{1}{4}$, the forepart must be rounded $\frac{1}{2}$ inch.

For the neck seam, draw a line from the shoulder point to the neck point, and divide it in three parts. Then starting from the shoulder, mark at one third, $1\frac{1}{8}$ in for the hollow of seam.

For the Scye, draw first a line from the end of shoulder seam to the front of scye, and mark in $\frac{1}{8}$ for the curve. Draw another line from the front of scye to the bottom of scye, at $4\frac{3}{4}$, and then mark in $\frac{7}{8}$ for the curve. Draw a third line from the bottom of scye to the side point, and mark in $\frac{3}{8}$ for the hollowing of scye.

For the side seam. Mark outside the line of construction, for the round of side seam, the same quantity that the back has been hollowed in from the oblique line, at the corresponding place. The curve must be drawn in a regular line through this point, and will generally cross

(Plate 3.)

the construction line a little above point 10.

For the waist seam. Draw lines from the centre point, to the bottom of side seam, and of front edge, and slightly curve the waist seam in from these lines.

For the Front Edge. Draw a regular curve from the top to the bottom, touching the front of chest at the level of the bottom of scye.

Of course this manner of drawing the curves, is only to be followed when beginning the system ; with a little practice the student will be able to draw the curves accurately, without any other guide than the eye, which soon learns the exact form required for the various seams.

We are now arrived at a point, at which many other systems of Cutting leave off. We have shown the student how to cut a standard or well-proportioned pattern, *which he can draft for any man, if he only knows his breast measure.* All men however, *are not* of the proportionate structure; some points of the standard pattern, are indeed, as we have seen, fixed and invariable for all sizes and structures, but we require some means of regulating the degree in which the other points should vary, for the different builds; and the only accurate means of ascertaining this, is *Measurement*, which we will now explain.

MEASUREMENT.

(Plate 4.)

The object of measurement is to learn the form and dimensions of the human body, and in order to attain this end in practice, it must consist of a short series of simple measures, which can be applied over any style of garment, without caring whether that garment is close fitting, or whether it fits well or badly.

We have devoted many years of careful study to this question of measurement, and have tried more than 100 different measures, taken to or from almost every point and part of a pattern, and we have only retained those in our system, that we have found to be thoroughly reliable.

The *Breast* and *Waist* are of course indispensible to rule these important parts of the

(Plate 3.)

pattern, and the points next in importance are the Lengths of Back and Forepart, and the Depth of Scye. A very slight amount of study will at once point out that these three last named measures of length, must all be taken *from one starting point,* because if a different starting point were taken for each of them, it would be quite impossible to make any comparison between them, and they would therefore be practically useless in the draft.

Besides this it will also be necessary to take a few other measures for those parts of a coat which, while they have nothing to do with the structure or balance, are nevertheless subject to variation, either by changes of Fashion, or to suit the special taste of the client.

There are also some disproportionate structures occasionally met with, that differ so much from the proportionate or Model type, that several additional measures are necessary, in order to attain perfect accuracy in the fit.

Our system of measurement therefore, which we have adopted after long and careful study,

(Plate 4.)

(*Plate* 4.)

is composed of TWO PRINCIPAL SERIES and a SUPPLEMENTARY one, each containing 6 measures only.

The First Series comprises the sizes and lengths, and shows at once whether the man is LONG or SHORT-BODIED, STOOPING or EXTRA-ERECT, THIN or STOUT WAISTED.

The Second Series, gives the measurement of all the parts which vary according to Fashion, or the taste of the client; such as the place of the hip buttons, the length of skirt, the size of sleeve, &c.

The Supplementary Series is always to be taken, whenever there is much deviation from the proportionate structure. This Series of measures gives the exact form and position of the arm-hole: it shows whether the chest is round or flat, and the shoulder blades flat or prominent; whether the shoulder is high or low, large or small.

We will now describe in detail these measures, and the manner of taking them, which are shown on figs. 1, 3, 4, 5, and 6 of *plate* 4.

FIRST SERIES, FIG. 1.

(*Plate* 4.)

No. 1 BREAST.—This measure is taken on the Waistcoat, *under the coat,* as shown on fig. 5. Place the tape horizontally, raising it up as high as possible under the arms, without raising it at the chest, and hold the tape with the thumb and forefinger of each hand. The tape must first be drawn very tight, and afterwards be loosened as the client breathes, so as to obtain the size of this part with the greatest accuracy. In writing it down we must only put the half; for instance, 18¾ inches for 37½, &c.

This measure indicates the graduated measure, to use in the draft. It is 18¾ in proportionate men.

No. 2 WAIST.—This measure is also taken under the coat: it goes round the body on a level with the hollow above the hips, see fig. 5, and it should be taken rather easy. Like the *breast* measure, it is only written down as half the length taken; say 15¾ for 31½ inches.

This measure, by comparison with the *breast,* shows if the waist is thin or stout. In the proportionate man it is 15¾ or 3 less than the breast.

(Plate 4.)

The three following measures, called *Curve, Bust,* and *Side,* Nos. 3, 4 and 5, fig. 1, are the special lengths required for our CENTRE POINT SYSTEM, by which we discover the exact structure of the client, and the true balance of the pattern to be drafted for him. The three measures all meet at a point, which is marked with chalk, at the waist level, in the hollow about 1 inch above the top of hip-bone, and which we call the CENTRE POINT (fig. 1, C. P.) The finding of this point, has hitherto depended upon great accuracy of calculation, for it is placed at *two-fifths* of the waist measure, from the seam in the middle of back, and this necessitated a calculation in the midst of measuring, or a reference to the Table on the right side page of plate 3, which many persons found to create a difficulty.

IMPROVED MEASURING TAPE.

We have therefore invented an IMPROVED TAPE MEASURE, on on the under side of which the distances of the *Centre Point* from the middle of back, are marked for all waists, thus doing away with all calculations. The divisions show the centre points, for half waists of 10, 11, 12, 13, 14, 15, 16, 17, &c., and so on to 30 inches, and the small marks between the divisions, show the centre points for waists of 10½, 11½, 12½, 13½, 14½, 15½, 16½, 17½, &c., and so on to 29½ waist.

At the other end of the tape is a 36-inch measure, starting from a eyelet hole near the end, to be used for taking accurately the *Curve* and *Bust* measures, as will be explained hereafter.

The right side of this tape, is merely the ordinary inch measure, 60 inches long, and used for taking the other measures of the customer. The loop at the end, is made to pass a pencil through (fig. 2), so that the tape may be held up tight under the arm, and the *Side* measure can then be taken with great accuracy. This Tape is further described on Plate 40.

———o———

The *Curve* and *Bust* measures, are the only measures which will really show the true balance a pattern should have, or in other words, which will give the exact relative lengths required for back

and forepart. Both these measures start from a PIVOT in the middle of back neck, at the top of back seam, and go to the CENTRE POINT, one passing in front of the arm, and the other at the back. The one in front of the arm is to be taken very tight, the other medium.

The *Curve* measure (No. 3) is really the length of back, but instead of going along the seam in the middle (where it is absolutely impossible to fix the place of the natural waist for all builds), it goes direct to the CENTRE POINT on the lip, which is fixed and invariable for all sizes and structures, and quite independent of changes of Fashion.

The *Bust* measure (No. 4) also starts from the top of back seam, and goes to the CENTRE POINT; but instead of going direct in a straight line, it passes over the shoulder in front of and under the arm, and really gives the true length of forepart. We will now describe how—

TO MARK THE CENTRE POINT (FIG. 6, C.P.)

First button the Coat, and press the body with the side of hand, just above the hips, to find the level of the hollow of waist, which is usually about 1 inch above the top of hip bone ; make a short chalk mark horizontally at this level. Next place the brass end of the tape at the middle of back, on the same level as the chalk mark, and measure by the scale on the tape, the distance of the CENTRE POINT from the middle of back, *according to the size of waist;* making a short chalk mark downwards at this distance, which with the first chalk mark will form a cross. *The middle of this Cross* is the CENTRE POINT.

N. B.—If the client is wearing a loose-fitting coat, such as the Paletot or a Jacket, the fronts must be drawn together, or laid over, and fastened by pins or by a tape tied round the waist, so as to have the garment perfectly tight-fitting at the back, and over the hips. This being done, the CENTRE POINT can be marked with as much accuracy as if the customer was wearing a dress-coat, and this is one great advantage of our especial System of Measurement.

(Plate 4.)

(*Plate 4.*)

TO FORM THE PIVOT (FIG. 6, P.)

The easiest way of taking the Curve and Bust measures is to form a pivot at the middle of back neck. To form this Pivot, take a large pin and stick it downwards into the coat at the top of back seam, leaving about ¼ inch of the head end out, so as to make a pivot on which to fix the tape, by means of the eyelet-hole in the Bust and Curve part of it: the measurer may then have both hands at liberty, and can take these important balance measures with great ease and certainty.

N.B.—If the neck seam in the coat the client is wearing, is placed too low at the back, its proper place must be marked with chalk on the stand of the collar, just above the seam in the middle of back, and the Pivot must then be formed at this point.

No. 3, CURVE.—Take the *Bust* and *Curve* *part* of the Tape, slip the eyelet-hole at the end of it over the head of the pin, and hold it there; the eyelet-hole must be exactly at the top of back seam : then with the other hand carry the tape perfectly straight to the CENTRE POINT, crossing the side seam near the middle, and not letting the tape be either very tight or too slack.

No. 4, BUST.—Continue to hold the end of the tape at the top of back seam, and with the other hand pass the tape over the shoulder in front of the arm, close to the front of scye, let-*ting the client's arm hang down in its natural*

(*Plate 4.*)

position; draw the tape very tight, to flatten any creases there may be at the front of arm, and carry it direct to the CENTRE POINT.

Now as the *Curve* and *Bust* measures both start from the top of back (a point which is always fixed and certain), and proceed to the CENTRE POINT, which is also fixed and certain for all sizes and structures ; the difference between these two measures must, it is evident, show the exact difference that there ought to be, between the lengths of back and forepart.

In a Proportionate man, the difference between these measures is 2½ : it is less than this for Stooping men, and more for Extra-erect men.

No. 5, SIDE.—Pass a pencil or penholder through the loop at the end of tape, and hold it tight under the arm (*the arm must not be raised up, but should lay close to the body*). Then measure the length to the CENTRE POINT, so as to ascertain exactly, the distance between this point and the bottom of scye.

This measure serves to rule the depth of the bottom of scye, and shows the degree in which

(Plate 4.)

it must be hollowed out below the side point, In proportionate men it is 8½, and is usually about half the length of back to natural waist. It is longer for extra erect men, and for small or high shoulders ; and less for stooping men, and for large or low shoulders.

No. 6, DEPTH OF SCYE. This measure, shown on fig. 1, starts from the same place as the *bust*, but instead of proceeding to the centre point, it stops at the level of the bottom of scye. To ascertain this level exactly, place a pencil or a penholder horizontally under the arm of the client, and measure down to the top of pencil. This measure must be taken very tight. The only use of this measure is to control or prove the accuracy of the two last measures. The *depth of scye and side* are really only the *bust* measure, taken in two parts, and if added together should produce the same quantity : for example in the proportionate structure:—

The depth of Scye is 12¾
And the side is 8½

Which is equal to the Bust, 21¼.

(Plate 4.)

When these three measures do not agree in this manner, there is evidently an error in one of them, and they must be measured over again.

SECOND SERIES, FIG. 3.

No. 7. LENGTH OF BACK TO HIP BUTTONS. Taken from the back neck, to the level of the top of back plaits. This measure is of course variable according to Fashion.

No. 8. LENGTH TO BOTTOM OF SKIRT. This is merely a continuation of the preceding measure, which is carried on from the notch to the bottom of skirt : its length is variable according to Fashion, taste, or the height of the client.

Nos. 9 and 10, WIDTH OF BACK, AND LENGTH OF SLEEVE. These measures are taken in the usual way; first raising the arm square with the body and bending it at the elbow. Then take the tape and place the end in the middle of back, opposite the hind arm seam ; measure first the width of back, according to fashion or the style of coat required ; and then continue the measure along the seam of the sleeve to the wrist.

(Plate 4.)

By deducting the width of back from the whole length, we obtain the true length of sleeve with great exactness.

The width of back is usually about 7½ graduated inches, for all sizes and structures, and the length to wrist is 32½ inches in the proportionate man; which, deducting the back 7½, leaves 25 for the real length of the sleeve. The length of arm is subject to great variation : it will however as a general rule, be found in proportion to the height of the man.

No. 11, ELBOW WIDTH.   Taken according to Fashion, or the wishes of the customer.

No. 12, WRIST.   Measured tight, medium, or loose, as required.   This measure, as well as the *Elbow*, should be written down as half, because it is only the half-measure that is used in drafting.

SUPPLEMENTARY SERIES, FIG. 4.

No. 13, *Back Stretch.*   Taken across the back, at the level of the bottom of back scye.   When we are taking this measure as part of the Supplementary Series, its accuracy becomes of great importance, and we have first to notice whether

(Plate 4.)

the coat the client is wearing, has the seam of the scye at its proper place.   If it is a *Paletot* or Paletot Jacket, the back stretch will probably be too wide ; if he has on a close-fitting coat of the old fashioned English cut, (in which the armhole is very large), it will be too narrow. The *true width* of back stretch, should be two-fifths of the breast measure, and this proportion should but rarely be deviated from.   It may however, be ⅜ more than this, for very stooping men, and ⅜ less for extremely erect ones.

No. 14, *Diameter of Arm.*   This measure gives the distance between the side point and the front of scye, and we obtain it by taking the tape between the thumb and forefinger of each hand :   then extend the other fingers square, those of one hand touching the front of arm, those of the other hand touching the back of arm, and with the eye make the length of tape equal to the real diameter of arm.

This measure is 5¼ in the proportionate structure.   It may be ½ inch more or less, according as the shoulders are large or small, forward or back-

(Plate 4.)

ward, but never exceeds this limit of variation.

No. 15, *Front of Scye.*   To take this measure we pass a pencil through the loop (fig. 2) and hold it against the front of arm with the thumb and forefinger of one hand ; then pass the Tape under the arm, and carry it on with the right hand, as to touch the middle seam of the back at the level of the bottom of back stretch, (fig. 4.)

In the proportionate man, the front of scye is 12¾, or equal to the back stretch 7½, and diameter 5¼, added together.

(It is important that the three last-named measures, Nos. 13, 14, and 15, should be taken with the greatest care and accuracy : and the student should practice taking them on the same man for some little time, and observe if the measures taken at different times are always alike. We generally find that there is at first, a tendency to take the *diameter* too small, and the *front of scye* too long.)

By the examination and comparison of these three measures, we can see at once what is the degree of round required to be given to the side seam.   In most cases, perhaps 70 out of every 100, the degree of roundness required is that indicated on fig. 1, *plate* 4.   But there are men whose structures vary in this point : some

---

(Plate 4.)

have the back round and the shoulder blades very prominent, while others have the back very flat and the blade bones hardly indicated.

Now in the proportionate man, we have seen that ;—

The Back Stretch 7½
Added to the Diameter....   5¼
                            ——
Is equal to the Front of Scye, 12¾

But if the man had a very round back, we should not find this calculation correct, because, while neither the *back stretch* nor the *diameter* would at all vary, the length of the *front of scye* would increase, because this measure passes over the prominence of the shoulder blades : we should then find :—

The Back Stretch 7½
The Diameter 5¼
                                 ——
And the Front of Scye 13¼, instead of 12¾

Showing that half inch more round than usual, is required on the side seam of forepart.

For a flat back, for an inverse reason, the

MEASUREMENT

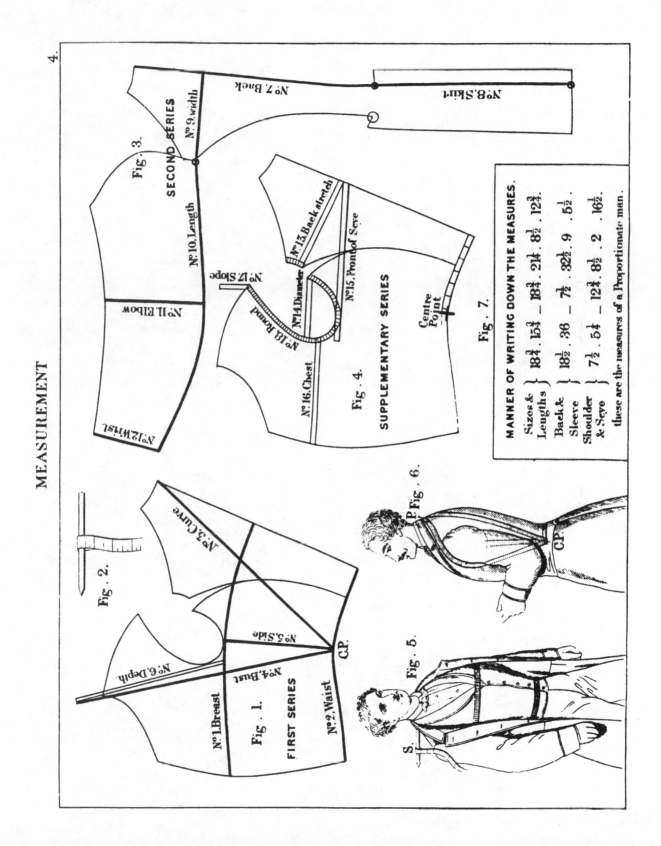

Fig. 3.

SECOND SERIES

No 9. width

No 10. Length

No 11. Elbow

No 12. Wrist

No 7. Back

No 8. Skirt

No 13. Back stretch

No 12. Slope

No 14. Diameter

No 15. Front of Seye

No 18. Round

No 16. Chest

Centre Point

Fig. 4.

SUPPLEMENTARY SERIES

Fig. 7.

MANNER OF WRITING DOWN THE MEASURES.

Sizes & Lengths	$18\frac{3}{4}$	$15\frac{1}{4}$	–	$18\frac{3}{4}$	$21\frac{1}{4}$	$8\frac{1}{2}$	$12\frac{3}{4}$
Back & Sleeve	$18\frac{1}{2}$	36	–	$7\frac{1}{2}$	$32\frac{1}{2}$	9	$.5\frac{1}{2}$
Shoulder & Seye	$7\frac{1}{2}$	$5\frac{1}{4}$	–	$12\frac{1}{4}$	$8\frac{1}{2}$	2	$16\frac{1}{2}$

these are the measures of a Proportionate man.

Fig. 2.

No 3. Curve

No 5. Side

No 6. Depth

No 4. Bust

No 1. Breast

Fig. 1.

FIRST SERIES

No 2. Waist

C.P.

P. Fig. 6.

C.P.

Fig. 5.

S.

(Plate 4.)

front of scye will be found *less,* than the back stretch and diameter added together, and *less* round must be given to the side seam.

No. 16, *Chest.* To take this measure well, hold the tape with the thumb and forefinger of each hand, and place the ends of the fingers against the front of each arm. We thus obtain the *whole* width of chest, which must be halved before writing it down. This measure is $8\frac{1}{2}$ in the proportionate structure, or 1 more than the width of back stretch. It will be shorter or longer, according as the shoulder is forward or backward, or the chest flat or prominent.

No. 17, *Slope.* The use of this measure, is to show the degree of slope required to be given to the top of shoulder. The manner of taking it is shown by fig. 5, S. Pass the pencil through the loop at the end of tape; place one end against the side of neck, and hold the pencil horizontally with one hand; then with the other hand measure the distance between the pencil and the top of shoulder.

The slope is 2 in the proportionate structure,

(Plate 4).

but it may vary to $2\frac{3}{4}$ for very low or sloping shoulders, or decrease to $1\frac{1}{4}$, 1, or even $\frac{1}{2}$ an inch, for very high shoulders. We hardly ever find shoulders more sloping than $2\frac{3}{4}$, and even this degree is not often met with. High shoulders are more frequently found, though they never have less slope than $\frac{1}{2}$ an inch, except in cases of deformity. Some men have one shoulder higher than the other, and for these the measures of both shoulders must be taken.

No. 18, *Round of Scye.* Measured round the armhole in the usual way, and serving to show whether the shoulders are large or small : it is therefore useful in some cases, as a guide for the *slope* of shoulder. It also may be used in the draft of sleeve. It is usually about $2\frac{1}{4}$ less than the *breast* measure in the proportionate structure : if there is a greater difference than this, the shoulder is *small*, if a less it is *large*.

In applying this measure to the pattern to prove the size of the armhole, care must be taken to deduct about $\frac{3}{4}$ of an inch for the stretching in front of scye.

HOW TO WRITE DOWN THE MEASURES.

(Plate 4.)

We have now described the complete series of measures which we consider necessary, and we have, at the bottom of *plate 4*, shown on fig. 7, the manner in which, when taking these measures, we write them down in three distinct lines, each containing one series.

In the *First line* we put first the Breast and Waist; then Curve, Bust, Side, and Depth of Scye.

In the *Second line.* Length to the hip buttons, ditto to the bottom of skirt; then Width of back, Length of wrist, Width of Elbow and Wrist.

In the *Third line* (when this series is taken), we put Back stretch, Diameter, Front of scye, Chest, Slope and Round of scye.

The FIRST series must always be taken in every case. The SECOND series may be taken or not, as preferred. The THIRD series should always be taken, whenever it is seen that there is any great deviation from the proportionate structure.

DRAFT TO MEASURE.

WITH THE FIRST SERIES OF MEASURES ONLY.

(Plate 5.)

The principles upon which the Draft to Measure is based, are extremely simple. In forming the pattern, we rule the dimensions of all the parts of the patterns which are given by the measures, according to the measures themselves. All the other points of the patterns, which are not given by the measures, and which do not vary according to the structure of the man, are ruled by the graduated measures, without any trouble whatever, copying the numbers of the proportionate pattern.

We may here observe, that in case all the measures should not have been taken, we must then rule the dimensions of those parts of the patterns for which the measures are wanting, by putting the figures of the proportionate pattern, with the graduated measures.

The draft to measure consists of four successive operations, which are shown on figs. 1 to 4,

(Plate 5.)

and for which the graduated measures and the common inch tape, are alternately employed in a regular fixed order, by which means the proper form required for each part of the pattern, is obtained in the simplest and most rapid manner possible.

The order in which the different parts of the pattern are formed on this *plate*, should always be retained in practice, because each part of the pattern is formed successively, until the draft is completed, and all confusion in the use or application of the measures is avoided.

FIRST OPERATION, FIG. 1; *Graduated Measures.*

Take first a Graduated Measure corresponding to the Breast measure of the client, and with it form a large square, which for all sizes and structures, must have a width of 23⅝ inches : then divide this square into two compartments, one having a width of 15¾, and intended to contain the forepart, and the other, which is for the back, having a width of 7⅞ graduated inches. Next mark for the shoulder point, 9½ from the

(Plate 5.)

construction line of the forepart, or 6¼ from the corner of the square : then mark 4 down, for corner of the square : then mark 4 down, for the slope of the neck seam, and 1½ in, for the top of front edge.

SECOND OPERATION, FIG. 2 ; *Common Inches.*

Starting from the right hand corner of the square, mark downwards for the top of back, the difference between the measures of *Bust* and *Curve.* This difference is called the *balance,* and its accuracy is of the greatest importance, because upon this depends the relative lengths of the back and forepart, and consequently the good fit of the pattern. Mark next from this point, the length of the back to the natural waist, which must be reckoned at 1½ graduated inches less than the length of the *Curve,* and draw a line square across to form the bottom of the square. We next rule the depth of the bottom of back stretch, by measuring downwards from the top, ¾ of a graduated inch more than a quarter of the length of back. We draw a line square across at this point, and continue

D

(Plate 5.)

it into the compartment for the forepart, to rule the height of the top of side point, which must be on the same level as the bottom of back stretch.

THIRD OPERATION, FIG. 3; *Graduated Measures.*

For the *Back*, mark first $2\frac{3}{8}$ graduated inches for the width of back neck; then $1\frac{1}{2}$ for the slope of the middle of back; $2\frac{3}{8}$ for the width of back at waist; and $1\frac{1}{8}$ up for the depth of the back scye. Next draw an oblique line from the bottom of back scye to the middle of back at waist, and draw by the hand, the curves of shoulder and side seams, as explained by fig. 1, *plate* 3. For the *Forepart:* Mark first on the construction line, 4 downwards for the slope of shoulder seam; then mark at $1\frac{1}{2}$ in for the place of the side point, or top of side seam, and make the width of scye $5\frac{1}{4}$. At the bottom of square, and starting from the line dividing the two compartments, mark at $4\frac{3}{4}$ for the place of the Centre Point, and at $6\frac{1}{2}$ for the Middle of Waist. Mark $1\frac{1}{4}$ *up* at these points, for the hollow of the hips, and draw a short line between them, and another

(Plate 5.)

line upwards from $4\frac{3}{4}$, for the place of the seam under the arm. Draw the curves of shoulder, and top parts of scye and side seams.

FOURTH OPERATION, FIG. 4; *Common Inches.*

Mark upwards from the hollow of the hip, the length of *Side* seam to measure; then starting from the *Middle of Waist*, (at $6\frac{1}{2}$ graduated inches), we rule the size of waist by putting half the measure in front, and half at the back, of course allowing for the width of back at waist. We generally give about $\frac{1}{4}$-inch less than the half measure at the back, so as to allow for the stretching at the bottom of side body, see fig. 2, *plate* 12. If the waist is thin, that is, more than 3 less than the breast, we draft the waist as for the proportionate structure, and reduce it as required, by taking out a fish in the forepart. Waists do not however, often require reducing in this way, even for thin men; because coats are now rarely made tight-fitting at waist. The pattern is completed, by drawing the remaining curves as explained on *plate* 3.

DRAFT TO MEASURE.

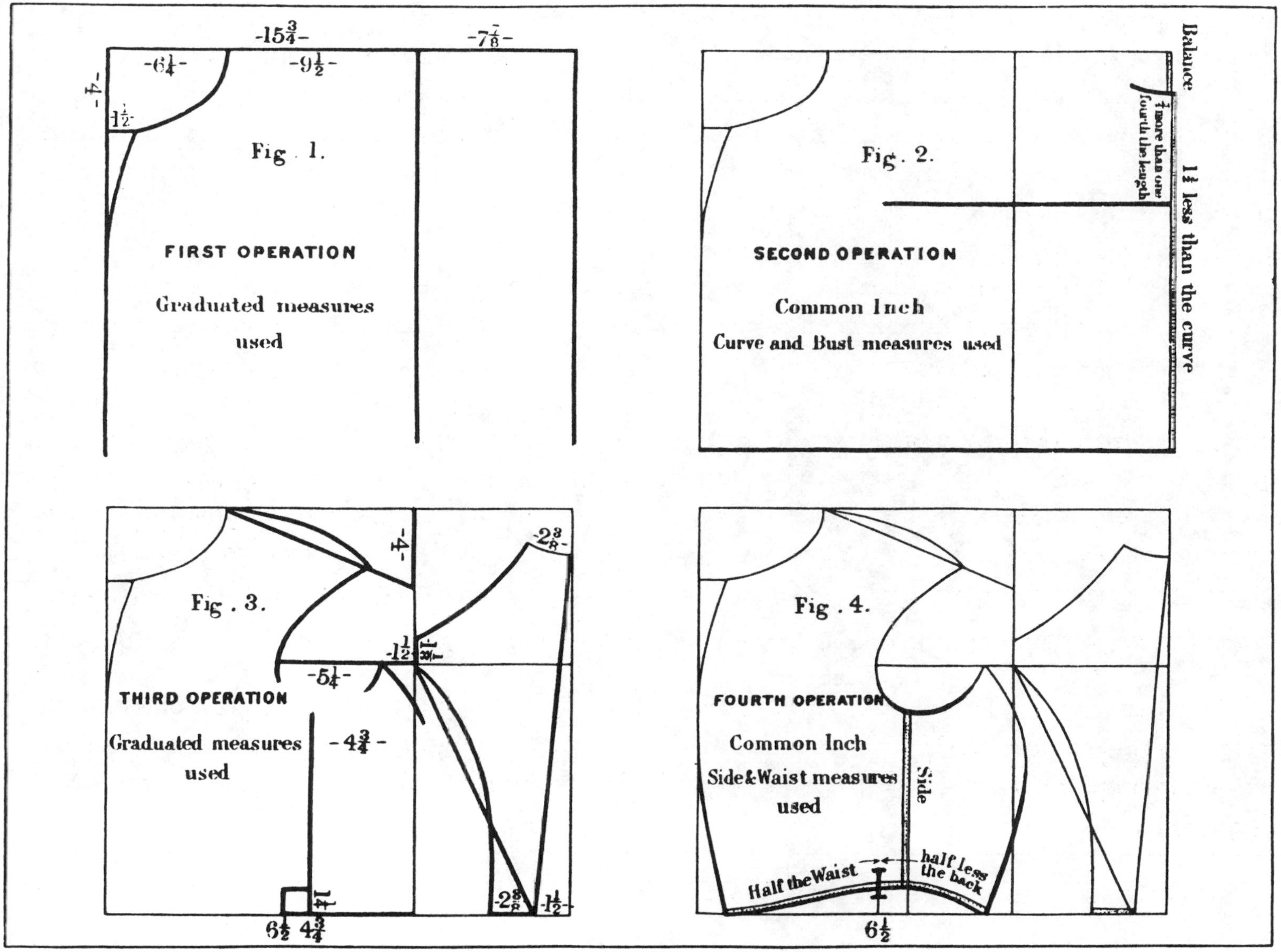
-15¾-
-7⅞-
-6¼-
-9½-
-4-
1½
Fig. 1.
FIRST OPERATION
Graduated measures used
Balance
1¼ less than the curve
¼ more than one fourth the length
Fig. 2.
SECOND OPERATION
Common Inch
Curve and Bust measures used
-4-
-2⅜-
Fig. 3.
-1½-
-5¼-
THIRD OPERATION
Graduated measures used
-4¾-
1¼
6½
4¾
-2⅜-
-1½-
Fig. 4.
FOURTH OPERATION
Common Inch
Side&Waist measures used
Side
Half the Waist
half less the back
6½

(Plate 5.)

The pattern thus drafted, is the wrapper or envelope of the body, and does not yet contain the various modifications required by Fashion. Before it becomes a finished pattern, we shall have to lengthen the waist more or less, to add the skirt and other pieces, according to the style of garment required, and perhaps to make some of the modifications in the place of seams, which are described hereafter.

The draft of sleeves, collars, and skirts, will be found on *plates 9* and *10*.

It will no doubt have been observed, that in forming this draft, we have only made use of the *first series* of measures, and for ordinary purposes this is all that is required. A cutter who worked the system solely with these few measures, would, with a little care, be successful in about three cases out of four, especially if he noticed if the client's shoulders were *high or low*, and gave less or more slope to the shoulder seam as required. When however, the client deviates from the proportionate standard, the *third series* will always be required, to produce an exact fit.

USE OF
THE SUPPLEMENTARY MEASURES.

(Plate 6.)

When the supplementary measures have been taken, the pattern as drafted on fig. 4, *plate 5*, will have to be *examined, and corrected* if required, by applying the measures of this series : this is done in a few minutes, and is explained by

FIG. 1.

First:—Apply the measure of *Back Stretch* to see if this part requires widening or narrowing, which will very rarely be the case.

Second:—Starting from the side point, apply the measure of *Diameter*, and take the front of scye forwarder or backwarder if required.

Third:—If the measure of *Front of Scye* is *more* than the *Back Stretch* and *Diameter* added together, give *more round* to the side seam of the forepart. If the *Front of Scye* measures *less* than these two measures, give *less* round to the side seam.

Fourth:—Starting from the front of scye at

(Plate 6.)

its corrected place, apply the width of *Chest*; and make the front edge rounder or flatter if required.

Fifth :—Correct the slope of shoulder, by marking downwards from 0 to S, (fig. 1,) double the length of *Slope* measure : for instance 4 for 2, 5 for 2½, 3 for 1½, &c. &c., so as to make the shoulder seam more sloping for low shoulders, and less sloping for high shoulders.

The pattern thus corrected, will be as perfect as possible, and will have the position of every point which is subject to variation, fixed by the measures themselves.

We will observe that the measures of the Third or Supplementary Series, may, if preferred, be used when forming the draft in the four operations of *plate 5*, by marking all the various points we have just described by the measures themselves, instead of marking them first by the graduated measures and afterwards correcting them if required. We must however recommend the plan we have just given to all beginners, because it is simpler and less liable to error.

THE VARIOUS CONFORMATIONS.

(Plate 6.)

We have now to show how this system of drafting adapts itself, without any trouble or difficulty, to all the changes of conformation which are met with in the human body. We shall therefore take each structure separately, and show how the application of the measures, causes the alterations in the pattern required for each build.

STOOPING AND EXTRA-ERECT STRUCTURES.

For the *Stooping* man, fig. 2 ; the difference between the measures of *Bust* and *Curve*, becomes less than for the proportionate structure, and this difference being placed at the corner of the square, causes the back to be much longer in comparison than the forepart. Besides this the chest will become flatter, and the side seam of forepart rounder ; which alterations are made by the supplementary measures.

N.B. In cases where the man is *Very Stooping*, we may also take the shoulder point a little forward, never more than ⅜, and lower

6

USE OF THE SUPPLEMENTARY MEASURES. THE DIFFERENT BUILDS.

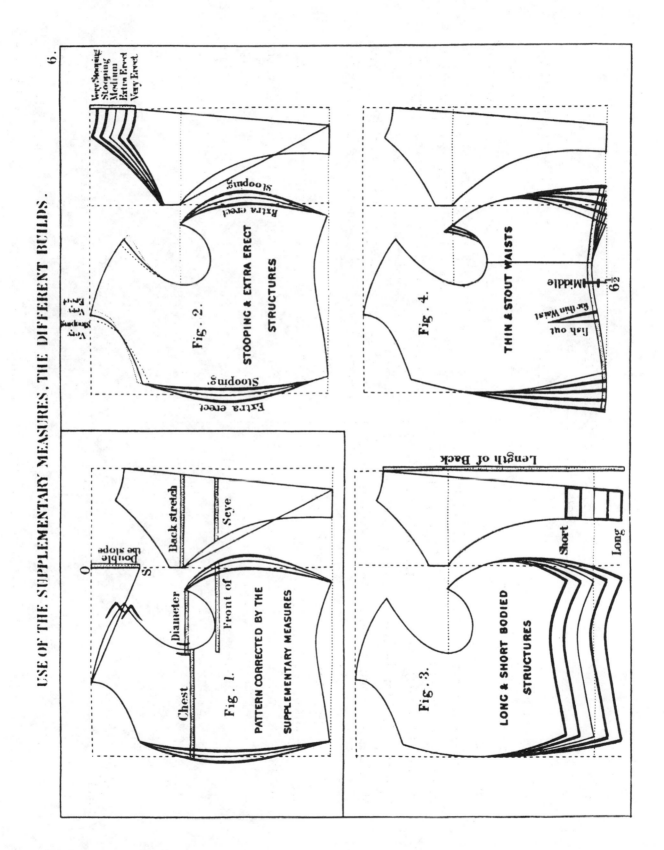

Fig. 1.
PATTERN CORRECTED BY THE
SUPPLEMENTARY MEASURES

Fig. 2.
STOOPING & EXTRA ERECT
STRUCTURES

Fig. 3.
LONG & SHORT BODIED
STRUCTURES

Fig. 4.
THIN & STOUT WAISTS

(*Plate* 6.)

the neck seam a little ; as shown by the interrupted line on fig. 2. This will improve the fit for these extreme cases, from the manner in which the "straight cut" in the forepart requires making up, (see *plate* 12.)

For the *Extra-Erect Man*, fig. 2; the back becomes shorter compared with the forepart, because the *balance* or difference between the measures of *Bust* and *Curve*, is more than for the Proportionate Structure. The supplementary measures also cause the chest to be made rounder, and the side seam plainer.

N.B. For *Extremely Erect* men, we may assist the fit, by taking back the shoulder piece and raising the neck seam a little—see the dotted line : but these variations in the place of the shoulder point, should only be made in extreme cases, and should never exceed ⅜ of an inch.

As a general rule in drafting for the Stooping and Extra-erect structures, we may say :—make the chest flatter and the side seams rounder for Stooping men, and give more round to the chest and less to the side seam of forepart, for Extra

(*Plate* 6.)

erect ones. This may be carried out in a slight degree for those builds, even when the supplementary measures have not been taken.

LONG AND SHORT BODIED STRUCTURES.

Fig. 3. The bottom of square being ruled by the length of back, (which is always taken as 1½ less than the *Curve* measure), the pattern will become of itself suited for the client, whether he is either a *Long or Short bodied* structure, or proportionate.

THIN AND STOUT WAISTS.

Fig. 4. In the proportionate man, the waist is 3 less than the breast : if the difference is *more* than this, the waist is thin ; if *less*, it is stout. For the *Thin Waist*, the front edge and side seams are drawn as for the proportionate structure, and the waist is diminished as required, by taking out a fish in the waist seam. If the *Waist* is *Stout* it is drafted correct at once, by giving half the measure in front and half at back, starting from the middle of waist. For

(Plate 6.)

Very Stout Waists the side point must be raised up and also advanced a little, as shown in this diagram: the reason will be found fully explained at page 124.

VARIATIONS IN SHOULDERS.

(Plate 7.)

The changes that are met with in the form of shoulders, require corresponding alterations to be made in the form of the scye. These changes seem at first rather complicated, but will be found very easy to understand, when classified under the three heads of *Depth, Height,* and *Width.*

Fig. 1, DEPTH. The depth of the bottom of scye may be more or less, if the shoulder is high or low, large or small. Its place is ruled exactly, by the measure of *Side.*

Fig. 2. HEIGHT. The slope of the line which rules the shoulder seam, varies according as the shoulders are high or low, because this slope of this line is always ruled at double the *Slope measure,* starting from 0 along the con-

(Plate 7.)

struction line. It sometimes is found not to be the same in the right and left shoulders of the client: when it varies, this part of the pattern must be drafted separately for each side.

Fig. 3. WIDTH. The scye may be forwarder or backwarder, if the shoulders are large or small, forward or backward. The exact position of the front of scye is ruled by the measure of *Diameter,* starting from the side point, which is always kept at a fixed base.

VERY STOOPING AND EXTREMELY ERECT PATTERNS.

We have now shown how our system adapts itself, to all the variations of structure which are met with in the human body; but before proceeding to describe the various modifications produced by Changes in Fashion, we will call the attention of our readers to figs. 4 and 5, in this *plate* 7, which are diagrams for the *Very Stooping and Extremely Erect* structures. We have given them side by side, to show in how perfect a manner, the system adapts itself to

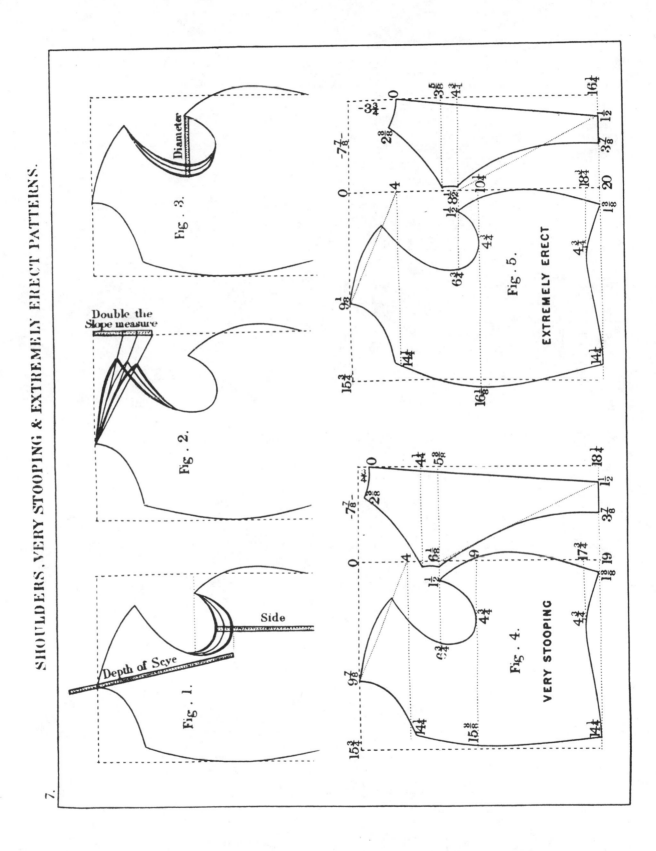

SHOULDERS. VERY STOOPING & EXTREMELY ERECT PATTERNS.

(Plate 7.)

these very dissimilar types. They will also be found a useful guide to the student, as to the extreme degrees of variation that are met with, especially as these structures, deviating more than any others from the proportionate standard, are the most difficult to draft.

CHANGES IN FASHION.

(Plate 8.)

Back without Seam in the Middle.

Fig. 1. The *balance*, or difference between the relative lengths of back and forepart, is ruled by the difference which exists between the measures of bust and curve. But, when drafting at once upon the cloth, if instead of placing the middle of back sloping as in the regular draft, it is desired to place the middle of back at the edge of square, so as to have no seam in the middle, the back is then displaced considerably, as shown by the strong line, and it is very important not to forget to raise up the top of back $\frac{3}{4}$ more than usual, as unless this is done, it will be found much too short at the

(Plate 8.)

top. Of course, at the bottom, it will also be $\frac{5}{8}$ higher up, than its usual place at the bottom of square : it is $\frac{5}{8}$ only, instead of $\frac{3}{4}$, thus showing that the back is $\frac{1}{8}$ longer, because it is placed straight instead of sloping. The bottom of back scye will also appear to be $\frac{3}{4}$ lower, as it is $5\frac{3}{4}$ instead of 5, measuring from the neck. The width of back stretch will then be $7\frac{1}{2}$, or $\frac{3}{8}$ less than the width of square, as shown on the diagram.

Neck Point Higher or Lower.

Fig. 2. This is an alteration often required by Fashion ; care however must be taken not to fall into extreme degrees, either of raising or lowering it. It should rarely be higher than 3, or lower than 5.

Back Wide or Narrow.

Fig. 2. The back if required may be made wider or narrower, provided that the same quantity which is added to or taken off from it, be compensated for in the side body, by either taking off or adding on equal quantities at the corresponding places, as shown on the diagram.

BACK NECK WIDE OR NARROW,
AND
BACK SCYE HIGH OR LOW.

(Plate 8.)

Fig. 3. As a general principle it will not matter if the places of the shoulder and side seams are varied, provided always that the quantity taken away from one piece is added to the other. For instance, the back neck may be wider, provided we make the shoulder strap of the forepart shorter to agree with it. The back scye may also be higher or lower, provided that a corresponding alteration is made in the side body, so as always to keep the side point on a level with the bottom of back scye.

We must say however, that these changes in the position of seams, should never be carried to extremes. There are certain places for the seams, which have been found by long experience to be those most suited for them, and these cannot be much deviated from in close fitting garments, without in some degree deranging the harmony of the cut.

LONG WAISTS.

(Plate 8.)

Fig. 4. The draft of the Long Waisted back and forepart, is made in the regular square, and consists in simply prolonging all the seams, any required quantity below the natural waist. For this lengthening, the front edge and side seams must be slightly sprung out, so as to make them parallel to the sides of the square. The seam under the arm must also be sprung out more or less, according to the prominence of the hips; this will, of course, make the forepart and side body lay over each other at the bottom, and they must be cut separate before laying the pattern on the cloth.

The figures at the bottom of the diagram, give an average or medium degree of lengthening. It will be seen that if the back is lengthened 2, the side body must be lengthened $2\frac{3}{8}$, or $2\frac{1}{4}$, because $\frac{3}{8}$ or $\frac{1}{4}$ an inch extra should always be allowed at this part, for the seam of back plait. The lengthening of the forepart, is usually a little less than that of the back.

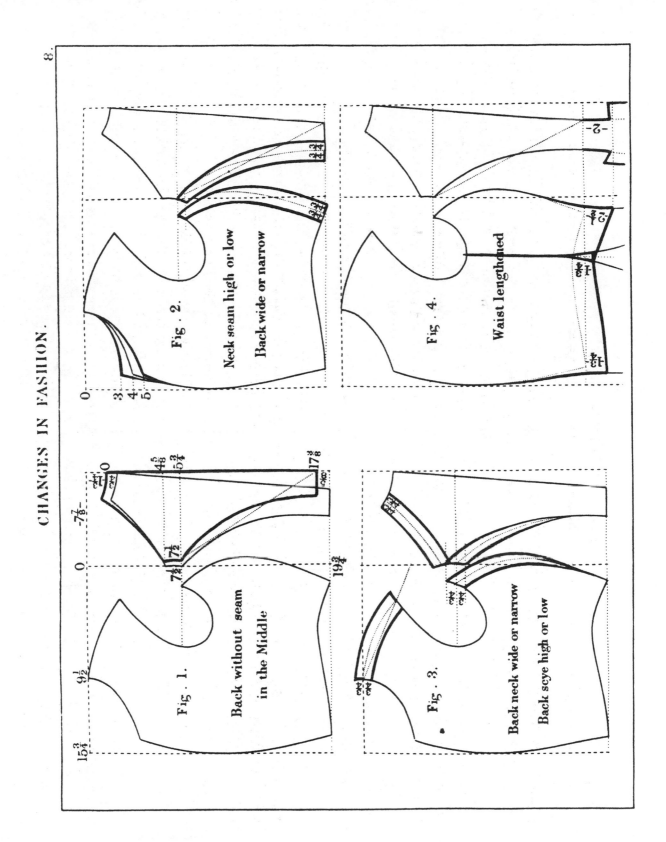

Fig . 1.

Back without seam
in the Middle

Fig . 2.

Neck seam high or low

Back wide or narrow

Fig . 3.

Back neck wide or narrow

Back scye high or low

Fig . 4.

Waist lengthened

ACCESSORY PIECES.

SLEEVES.

(*Plate* 9.)

For the Draft to Measure we proceed as follows:—

Fig. 1. Draw first the *Line of Construction*: then take a graduated measure corresponding to the breast measure of the client, and starting from 0, measure along the line—$1\frac{1}{8}$ for the top of hind arm seam, and $4\frac{3}{8}$ for the top of forearm. Draw lines square across from 0 and $1\frac{1}{8}$, and then for the widths, mark across from 0,—5 for the top of sleeve head, and from $1\frac{1}{8}$,—first $2\frac{1}{4}$ for the curve, and then $8\frac{5}{8}$ for the width of the top.

Fig. 2. Where the *Round of Scye* measure has been taken, correct the width of the top of sleeve, by putting across from $1\frac{1}{8}$, *half* the above measure with $\frac{3}{8}$ added; say $8\frac{5}{8}$ (or $8\frac{1}{4}$ *plus* $\frac{3}{8}$) for a measure of $16\frac{1}{2}$. The reason for adding this $\frac{3}{8}$, is that it is always best to cut the under side of sleeve, a little less at top, see fig. 3.

Fig. 2. Next mark along the construction line from $1\frac{1}{8}$, the *Length of Sleeve* to measure, (*Plate* 9.) and from this point mark back from $1\frac{1}{4}$ to $1\frac{1}{2}$ graduated inches, for the slope of wrist. Mark for the height of elbow at half the length of forearm seam, and draw lines square across at elbow and bottom. On the elbow line; mark in according to Fashion, any quantity (not exceeding 2 graduated inches) for the curve of forearm seam. Lastly, put the widths of Elbow and Wrist according to measure, or to Fashion. The Curves are all drawn by the hand.

Standard Sleeve.

Fig. 3, gives the pattern of a tight fitting sleeve for a proportionate man. When no measures have been taken for this piece, we draft this proportionate sleeve by a graduated measure, and afterwards make any of the modifications required by fashion, shown on fig. 4.

Various Styles.

Fig, 4. The *forearm seam* may be perfectly straight on the construction line, or curved as required. The *hind arm seam* may either be at $8\frac{5}{8}$, which is the least width that should be given, or any extra quantity may be allowed, as

(Plate 9.)

shown by the strong black lines, so as to make the sleeve very wide at elbow. The width at *Wrist* may also vary considerably. It must never be less than $4\frac{3}{4}$, and any extra quantity may be allowed, but only at the hind arm seam, as shown by the interrupted line. For the present style of sleeve, see *plate 2, fig. 3.*

LAPELS.

The draft of the lapel is made by taking as a construction line, the front or outside line of the regular square, and the position of this line can always be ascertained, by drawing two lines square to each other and placing the shoulder point at $6\frac{1}{4}$ and the front of neck seam at 4, as shown on figs. 5, 6, and 7. To draft a lapel, take this line as a base, give to the lapel the same length as the front edge of forepart, except for Dress Coats, which are cut longer at the bottom than the forepart, to allow for the depth of the strap of the skirt: then mark the widths at top, middle, and bottom, according to fashion or the particular style required.

Fig. 5. Lapels for *Double Breasted Coats,*

(Plate 9.)

such as Dress, Frock, and Newmarket Coats, are cut separate, as shown by this diagram. The upper part of sewing on edge, may be cut round if preferred, as shown by the dotted line.

The place of the buttons is always marked from the edge of forepart, at 1 inch less than the width of lapel at the corresponding place.

Fig. 6. For *Single Breasted Coats, Jackets, &c.,* the lapel is cut in one piece with the forepart, without any other seam than the fish taken out in the neck; the lapel may be curved in a little at the waist, to take off a part of the superfluous width, which there would otherwise be at this part. The usual way of taking out the fish, in the neck, is shown by the plain line. Some cutters however, raise up the neck a little, and take out another small V crosswise, at the bottom of the large one, as shown by the open dotted line; others take out the fish in the middle of neck seam, (as shown by the fine dotted line).

Fig. 7. Even in close fitting garments, such as double-breasted Frock Coats, &c., the lapel may be joined completely to the front edge of

SLEEVES AND LAPELS.

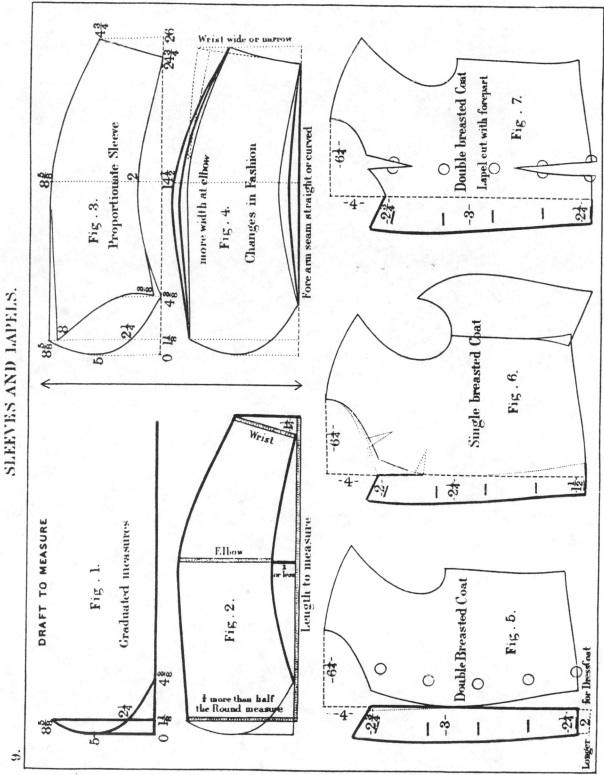

DRAFT TO MEASURE

Fig. 1.

Graduated measures

Fig. 2.

Wrist

Elbow

¾ more than half the Round measure

Length to measure

Fig. 3.

Proportionate Sleeve

more width at elbow

Fig. 4.

Changes in Fashion

Wrist wide or narrow

Fore arm seam straight or curved

Single breasted Coat

Fig. 6.

Double breasted Coat

Lapel cut with forepart

Fig. 7.

Double Breasted Coat

Fig. 5.

Longer ⋅ 2 ⋅ for Dressfoot

9.

(*Plate 9.*)

the forepart, but then we must replace the round given to the chest, by two fishes at the button line, one at the neck and another at waist. This form is of all others the easiest to make up, since the cut naturally places the roundness of the chest in the required place.

COLLARS.

(*Plate 10.*)

Fig. 1. To draft a collar, we must first draw the *Crease Line.* This line always touches the corner of shoulder piece, and crosses the lapel seam at a place which will be higher or lower, according as the turnover is required to be long or short. Starting from this line, we mark below it the height of the stand, and above it the depth of the fall, according to Fashion: the curve of the front part of collar, should always follow the neck seam of the forepart for about 4 inches. The length is ruled by the neck seam of forepart and the back neck, with about ½ inch extra allowed; this extra ½ inch is not to be worked up, but is merely an allowance in case of errors.

Fig. 2, gives a collar of the present Fashion

(*Plate 10.*)

(1868), to be drafted by the graduated measures.

On this diagram, fig. 2, we have also shown how collars may be modified in shape, to suit either very short or very long turnovers. For *short turnovers*, the back part of the collar must be curved upwards from the usual construction line, as shown by the fine dotted line. For *long turnovers*, on the contrary, the collar must be curved downwards, like the interrupted line.

SKIRTS.

FROCK COATS.

Fig. 3. The skirts of Frock Coats are traced in a precisely similar manner, no matter what may be the degree of fullness. The principle is this:—Draw first the construction line, and make a mark across at 0 for the place of the waist seam. Rise up above this any quantity, as shown on the diagram, according to the degree of fullness required, and draw a line square across at this point. Then mark in from 0, $\frac{3}{4}$ for the turning in at front edge, and rule the length of the top of skirt according to the size

(*Plate* 10.)

of waist. To find the spring of back plait, place the side body on the top of skirt, as shown by the dotted line, and continue the back of skirt in the same line as the bottom of side. The length of the skirt is ruled to measure or to Fashion, giving at front $\frac{3}{4}$ less length than at back, and the curve at the bottom is drawn by the hand. Some Cutters always slope off the back plaits a little at the bottom so as to reduce the fullness, as shown by the dotted line.

Fig. 4, shows all the various degrees of fulness, which may be given to these skirts. The least degree is $1\frac{1}{2}$, and the greatest is 9, which is now only used for some Foreign Uniforms.

SHOOTING COATS,

These skirts are cut as shown by fig. 3, giving a slope of 3 at the top. They are shorter than Frock Coat skirts, and have the front edge sloping, and the corner rounded off more or less, according to Fashion. The size, length, &c., are ruled as for a Frock coat.

DRESS COATS.

Fig. 5, shows the manner of drafting Skirts

(*Plate* 10.)

for Dress Coats. The construction line is here placed at the back, instead of the front edge. For Dress coats worn unbuttoned, give a slope of $1\frac{1}{2}$ to the top of skirt: for Dress coats worn buttoned, a slope of 3; next mark the width of top of skirt, according to the size of waist of the forepart and side body, rule the length of Skirt to measure, and put the widths of skirt and length of strap, according to Fashion.

OXFORD AND NEWMARKET COATS.

Fig. 5. For *Oxford Coats*, the skirts are sloped 3 at the top; the length is ruled to measure, and the rest of the skirt to Fashion.

Skirts for *Newmarket Coats*, have a slope of from 3 to 4 at the top, according as the coat is cut away, or is intended to be worn buttoned at the waist: the length is ruled to measure, and the rest of the skirt is shaped to Fashion.

N.B. Any of the skirts on fig. 5, may, (if more fullness is wanted at the hips) have two small fishes taken out at the top, as shown by the dotted lines.

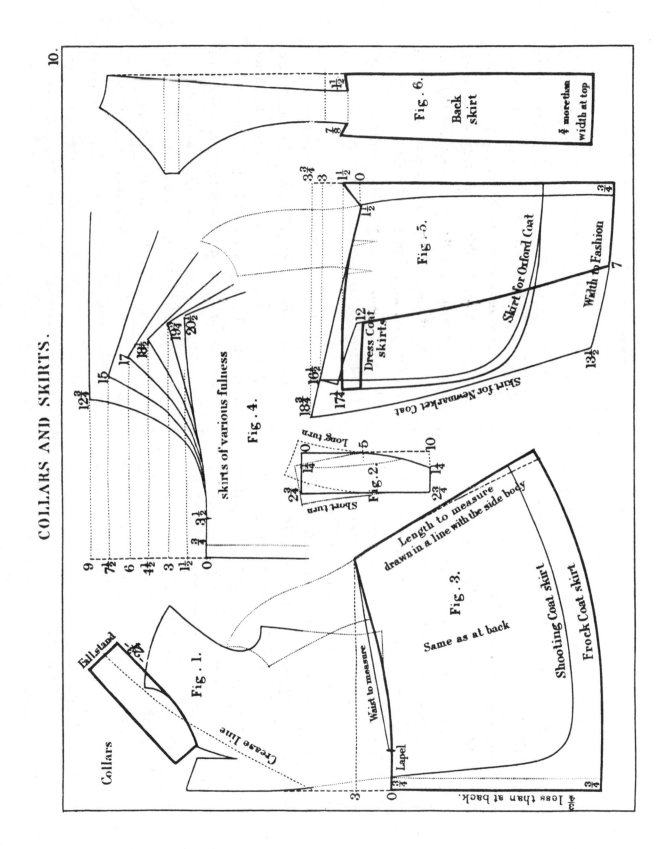

COLLARS AND SKIRTS.

10.

Fig. 6.
Back skirt
¼ more than width at top

Fig. 5.
Skirt for Oxford Coat
Dress Coat skirts
Skirt for Newmarket Coat
Width to Fashion

skirts of various fulness
Fig. 4.

Fig. 2.
Long turn
Short turn

Fig. 3.
Length to measure drawn in a line with the side body
Same as at back
Shooting Coat skirt
Frock Coat skirt
Waist to measure
Lapel
¼ less than at back.

Fig. 1.
Collars
Crease line
Fallstand

(*Plate 10.*)

Back Skirts.

Fig. 6. Back Skirts are always formed in the same manner. Add at the side seam, ⅞ for the plait, and rule the length by that of the front skirt: the width at bottom is marked at from ½ to 1½, more than the width of top, according to Fashion. For the present Fashion, ¾ of an inch is about the usual allowance,

JACKETS OR MORNING COATS.

(*Plate 11.*)

A Jacket or Morning Coat, is a garment which has the skirt cut in one piece with the forepart, so as to show no waist seam at the front.

The draft for this style, is shown on figs. 1 and 2. First draw the close fitting forepart to measure in the regular square, but giving an extra width of about 4 or 5 inches to the compartment of the back, so as to allow room for the fullness of skirt at the bottom, without one piece laying over another.

Fig. 2. The back and back skirt are formed in the usual way, lengthening the waist as required.

Fig. 1. For the forepart, add in front of the

(*Plate 11.*)

square a width of from 2 to 3 inches, or less according to Fashion, for the Lapel, and draw the front edge parallel to the edge of square, for a *Morning Coat*, which is the style that buttons to the waist. If for a *Jacket*, slope the front edge off to any degree, as shown on fig. 1. The waist is lengthened as usual, and the skirt is drafted in the usual way at the bottom of forepart, by drawing the top square with the construction line for a plain skirt, or sloping it up a little for a fuller skirt, as shown by the interrupted line. The spring of back plait is ruled in the same way as for a Frock coat skirt. Care must be taken to lengthen the waist of the side body, a little more than that of the forepart, so as to allow for the seam at the waist. The seam under the arm is also usually cut sloping, the bottom being at 5¾, the dotted line shows the place of this seam in the regular draft.

Morning Coats for Very Stout Waists.

We have just said that for Morning Coats the front edge is to be drawn parallel to the edge

(*Plate* 11.)

of square; there is however, one exception to this rule, namely Morning Coats for very stout men, shown on fig. 3. For very stout waists the bottom of front edge goes beyond the square, as shown by fig. 4, *plate* 6. Consequently if the front edge was drawn parallel to the edge of square, the coat would really be a Jacket very much cut away, and could not button at the waist. In this case then, the lapel must be drawn sloping so as to agree with the front edge of forepart, and this will enable us to dispense with the usual fish at the neck, which is required for medium or small waists.

LARGE SIZED PATTERN.

Fig. 4 is a Back suited for the above Forepart, fig. 3. These patterns will be found useful for the very large sizes; they may be drafted by the graduated measures, being the most usual structure that is met with for very stout men.

MAKING UP.

(*Plate* 12.)

Fig. 1 gives the form of *Front Lining* which we recommend: in it the roundness for the chest

(*Plate* 12.)

is obtained by large fishes, taken out in the neck and waist seams.

Fig. 2. In *Making Up* our patterns require a little STRETCHING and FULLING, at the parts indicated on this diagram. The Back will generally require fulling or tightening at the shoulder and upper part of side seams. The Forepart will require stretching just above the front of scye, and at the shoulder and neck seams, so as to take away the creases which sometimes form at the hollow in front of shoulder. A little stretching may also be given at the bottom of side body. A good deal of fulling is required at the front edge, to give the round for the chest, and it is most usual to take out small fishes at this part as shown on fig. 7.

Figs. 3 and 4. The degree of fulness required, in the shoulder and side seams of back, will vary according to the place of the seams. If these seams are nearly straight, fig. 3, they must be very much fulled. If they are a good deal curved, see fig. 4, they must be made up plain. Many Cutters have adopted for their coats,

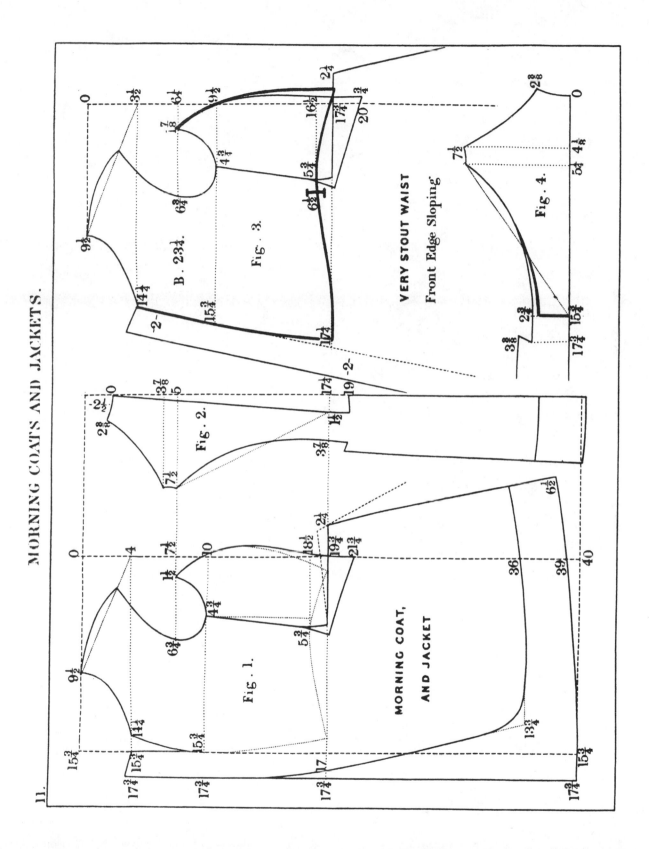

MORNING COATS AND JACKETS.

(Plate 12.)

foreparts with the shoulder pieces much more forward or backward, than in our system; and figs. 5 and 6 show the manner in which they are obliged to be made up, and by which the shoulder point is really brought back to the place at which we have fixed it; thus proving that these extremes of straightness or crookedness, merely create extra difficulties for the workman.

STRAIGHT CUT, fig. 5. For this cut the neck seam must be a good deal stretched, so as to bring back the shoulder piece to its proper place.

This has not a bad effect in some cases, when used with discretion, especially for thin men with large shoulders. Care must be taken however, when straightening a shoulder piece, to cut it a trifle shorter, for this reason:—The length of shoulder strap must agree with the measure of *Depth of Scye:* now if we take the bottom of this measure as a pivot, and describe an arc of a circle, we at once see that when we straighten the shoulder piece, we must, at the same time, also shorten it, or it will become too long. CROOKED CUT, fig. 6. For this form we must

(Plate 12.)

take out extra fishes in the neck and front edge, and also stretch the scye hard, so as to bring the shoulder piece back to its real place. This cut may be used with advantage, if a very great degree of roundness is required at the chest.

Fig. 7. Shows how a long waisted coat, may be cut with fish under the arm, so as to avoid the forepart and side body laying over each other at the hip. To do this, we raise up the side point, at the same time advancing it a little more beyond the construction line, as shown by the dotted lines, which give the usual position of side body, while the black lines show the side body drawn in its new position.

In this pattern the fish at waist being $\frac{3}{4}$, the side point is raised up $\frac{3}{8}$ of an inch and advanced $\frac{1}{4}$ of an inch, viz. to $1\frac{3}{4}$. Many Cutters prefer this manner of drafting, because the side body can then be cut separate at once without joining on a piece at the bottom: we have therefore again returned to this subject in our remarks on Paletots, plate 26, fig. 3, and have given some further explanations respecting it.

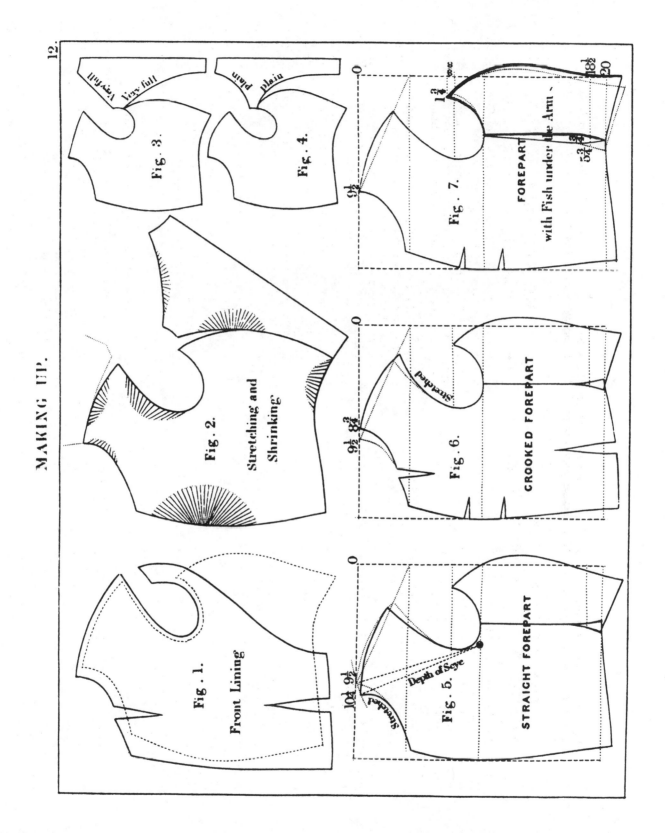

MAKING UP.

Fig. 1.
Front Lining

Fig. 2.
Stretching and
Shrinking

Fig. 3.

Very full

Fig. 4.

plain

Fig. 5.
STRAIGHT FOREPART
Depth of Scye

Fig. 6.
CROOKED FOREPART
Stretched

Fig. 7.
FOREPART
with Fish under the Arm

HANDBOOK OF PRACTICAL CUTTING.

PART THE SECOND.

WAISTCOATS.

(Plate 13.)

In commencing the study of this branch of our subject, we will observe that the draft of Waistcoats is much simpler than that of coats, and there are fewer difficulties to overcome. A Waistcoat may be considered more as an ornament than a garment, as it is only the front of it which is seen, and if this part has the proper balance, and the proper degree of roundness required for the chest, the fit of the back is of minor importance. So much is this the case that it is often possible for a man to wear a waistcoat much too large for him, without appearing ridiculous, and this fact is often taken advantage of by the ready-made houses.

(Plate 13.)

The front however, being of the most importance, it becomes all the more necessary that this part should be cut with the greatest degree of accuracy that can be obtained, leaving all the extra quantities required for ease, comfort, and the various motions of the body, to be given in the back.

We have devoted much time and study to the consideration of this subject, and the system here given, is we think, arranged to produce a pattern having all the characteristics we have named above: the fronts will be found to lay perfectly even on the body, and sufficient width is allowed across the middle, to give an appearance of breadth to the chest of the client. The back has the exact degree of extra fulness necessary, without being too large in any part,

(Plate 13.)

or forming ungraceful creases. A few creases of course there must be, because the back of a Waistcoat is a flat piece of stuff, which has to cover a round part of the body, and allowances must be made for ease, and for the movements of the arm, shoulder, and back; but these are all calculated for, and are arranged so as not to cause the least inconvenience.

THE
PROPORTIONATE PATTERN.

Figs. 1 and 2, give the MODEL TYPE, or PROPORTIONATE PATTERN of a Waistcoat. It is for a man having the same measures as for the Coat in Part 1, figs. 1 and 2, *plate 2*, and all the general remarks that we made about that diagram, apply equally to this pattern. It may be drafted for any size by the graduated measures, and is that which will fit the greatest number of persons: it will, therefore, be the oftenest required. The student must learn by heart all the figures of this diagram, so as to be

(Plate 13.)

able to draft it at once if required, without the book. These figures are very simple, and in a few words we will call attention to them, and will explain some of the principal differences which exist between the Waistcoat and the Coat pattern.

We will remark first,—that in this pattern the lengths of back and of forepart to the bottom of side seam, are both 18¾, while in a coat there is a difference of 2½ between these lengths.

This difference arises from several causes: *first* —because the back of the Waistcoat is made lower at the waist, so as to afford warmth and protection to the loins: *second*—because the back neck is cut a little higher, as the collar of a Waistcoat is made so much lower: *third*— because of the *extra* length which the back of a Waistcoat must have, to allow of the various movements of the body being made without deranging the front. All these reasons combined, cause the back to become relatively longer, and so equalize the lengths of the two pieces in the proportionate structure.

The Forepart, Fig. 1.

(*Plate* 13.)

The *total length* is $21\frac{1}{4}$, and the length to bottom of side is $18\frac{3}{4}$; the difference between these lengths, gives $2\frac{1}{2}$ for the slope of waist, which is, we may observe, exactly equal to the width of back neck. These lengths will of course vary, if the man is long or short bodied.

The *bottom of Scye* is at $10\frac{1}{4}$, which deducted from $18\frac{3}{4}$, gives $8\frac{1}{2}$ for the length of side seam, or exactly the length of *Side* measure $8\frac{1}{2}$ (see page 11). This may at first seem an error, because the scye of a Waistcoat ought to be cut lower than that of a coat: it is, however, perfectly correct, because the bottom of the Waistcoat, from which the side is measured, is nearly $\frac{3}{4}$ of an inch lower than the natural waist of the Coat, the turning in at the bottom being allowed for in the draft.

The *hollowing out of Scye* is at $7\frac{1}{2}$, or $2\frac{3}{4}$ above the top of side seam. It is always at this height above the bottom of scye, for all sizes and structures.

(*Plate* 13.)

The *bottom of neck seam* is at $4\frac{3}{4}$, for the style buttoning up to the top, but this will be of course, lower for other styles of Waistcoat, and depends solely on Fashion.

The *slope of neck seam* is at 2, and this is always a fixed degree for all cases.

The *shoulder point* is at $5\frac{3}{4}$, and should never vary from this proportion, unless the forepart is deranged by fishes (see *plate* 16.)

The *neck point*, or top of front edge is at 10.

The *front of scye* is at $2\frac{3}{4}$ in all cases.

The *width of chest* is $10\frac{5}{8}$: this width is rarely subject to variation; it may, however, be $\frac{3}{8}$ more for extremely round chested men, and $\frac{3}{8}$ less for very flat chests (see fig. 5, *plate* 14).

The taking in of the *bottom of side* is $1\frac{1}{2}$, and is always at this distance in all cases.

The *front of waist* is at $9\frac{1}{4}$, but may be more or less according as the waist is Stout or Thin.

The Back.

The *length and the bottom of scye*, $18\frac{3}{4}$, and $10\frac{1}{4}$, are the same as in the forepart, for the

(Plate 13.)

proportionate structure; they will, however, both become more for Stooping men, and less for Extra-erect ones, the length of side seam being always kept equal to that of the forepart.

The *slope of shoulder* will, in almost all cases be a fixed point at 3½. It may however, vary for high or low shoulders.

For the widths.—The *back neck* (2½); the *widths of back stretch* (7¼), and *bottom of scye* (10⅝), are fixed points in all cases. *The width of waist* is at 9¼ in the Proportionate Structure.

From the foregoing description, it will be at once seen that, just the same as for Coats, all those points subject to variation, should be marked according to the Measures taken on the client, and those points which are fixed and invariable for all sizes and structures, are to be Marked by the Graduated Measures.

HOW TO
DRAW THE CURVES.

The Curves of a Waistcoat are very simple, and very easy to learn.

(Plate 13.)

In the FOREPART. The *neck seam* is hollowed 1 graduated inch, at 2¼ from the shoulder point. The *shoulder seam* is rounded ¼ inch, and the *side seam* hollowed ¼ inch. The *scye* is hollowed ⅜ at the top, and ⅞ at the bottom, from straight lines drawn from the front of scye, to the shoulder and the bottom of scye.

In the BACK. The *back neck* is curved up ⅜; the shoulder and side seams are each hollowed in ¼ inch: the upper part of *scye* is drawn square with the dotted construction line, and the lower part is hollowed in 1½, from a line drawn from the top to the bottom of back scye.

These curves are always to be drawn in the same manner, for all sizes and structures; of course using the graduated measures, for all sizes larger or smaller than 18¾ breast.

VARIATION IN STRUCTURES.

Figs. 5 and 6, show some of the principal variations required in Waistcoats, to suit the various conformations.

WAISTCOATS.

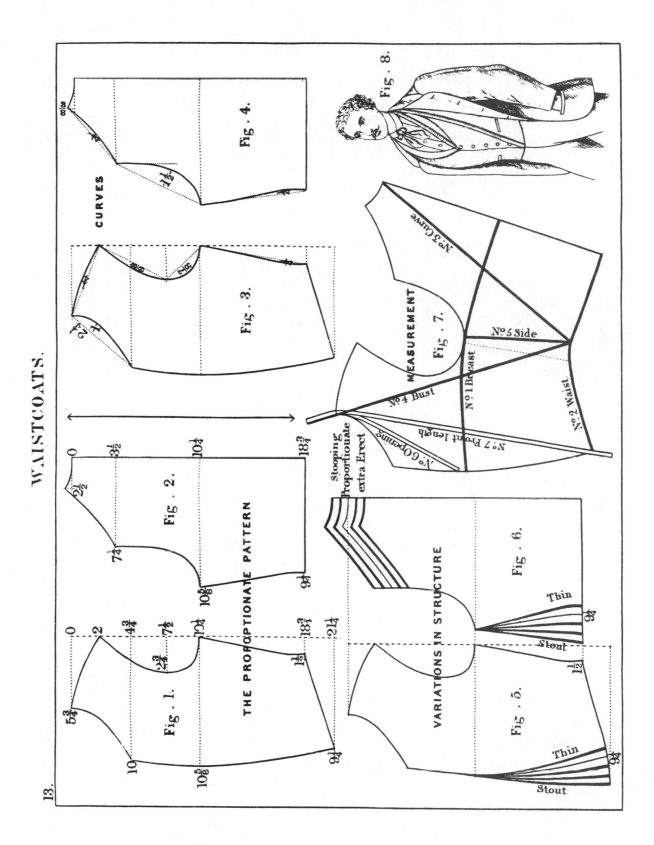

13.

THE PROPORTIONATE PATTERN

Fig. 1.

Fig. 2.

CURVES

Fig. 3.

Fig. 4.

VARIATIONS IN STRUCTURE

Fig. 5.

Fig. 6.

Thin

Stout

Stooping
Proportionate
extra Erect

MEASUREMENT

Fig. 7.

Nº 3 Curve

Nº 5 Side

Nº 1 Breast

Nº 4 Bust

Nº 2 Waist.

Nº 7 Front Length

Nº 6 Opening

Fig. 8.

MEASUREMENT.

(Plate 13.)

In taking the measures of a Waistcoat, we have, even for very disproportionate structures, much fewer points to ascertain than for a coat. The scye of a Waistcoat is so large, that we need take no measures for the shoulder, and the only ones indeed that are required, are shown on fig. 7: they are the *first five measures* of the First Series, as described for coats, and shown on Figs. 7 and 8, viz.:—

Breast, Waist, Curve, Bust, and Side.

If the customer is very particular as to the exact style required, we may add, as supplementary measures, the *Depth of Opening*, and the *Length to bottom of Front.*

If the client is ordering a coat and waistcoat at the same time, there are, of course, no measures required to be taken for the waistcoat, except, perhaps, Nos. 6 and 7. But if as sometimes happens, the customer requires a waistcoat only, then the first five measures must be taken, in the same manner as for a coat, and

MEASUREMENT.

(Plate 13.)

The back, as compared with the forepart, may be required to be made higher or lower, according as the client is *Stooping* or *Extra-erect*, and unless this alteration is correctly made, the pattern can not have the proper balance, and must fit ungracefully.

The *Thin Waist* requires the pattern to be sloped off at the front of waist in the forepart, and at the bottom of side seam in the back. *Stout Waists*, on the contrary, require extra allowances given at these places, according to the size, half being given to the front and half to the back. It should be observed that for *Stout* waists, the extra allowance in the front, is sloped off to nothing at the height of the breast line, and also that the side seam of the back, is, for *Stout* men, drawn in a straight line.

The variations we have indicated on these diagrams, show at a glance how indispensible for accuracy in the cut of Waistcoats, is Measurement, which we will now proceed to explain.

(Plate 13).

will be found fully explained in Part 1, pages 9 to 12, and *plate* 4.

No. 1, BREAST. Taken on the Waistcoat.

No. 2, WAIST. A little tighter than for a coat : say 15½ for the proportionate man.

No. 3, CURVE. From the top of back to the centre point, as for a coat.

No. 4, BUST. As for a coat. N.B.—In taking the *bust* and *curve* measures over a loose fitting coat, the fronts must be laid over and drawn together, so as to make the coat fit close at the back ; unless this is done, the centre point cannot be marked at its proper place, and the *Curve* may be taken too short and the *Bust* too long.

No. 5, SIDE. As for the coat, except that it need not be taken up quite so high; as it is of no importance in a Waistcoat, if the scye should be a little lower.

No. 6, *Opening*, or length of neck seam, from the middle of back neck to the top button, measured neither too tight nor too slack, see figs. 7 and 8.

(Plate 13.)

No. 7, *Front Length*. Measured from the centre of back neck, to the bottom of front. See figs. 7 and 8.

DRAFT TO MEASURE.

(*Plate* 14.)

The front of a Waistcoat being cut in the material, and the back only in lining, we draft the two pieces separately, instead of placing them side by side in two squares, as for coats.

THE FOREPART.—FIGS. 1 & 2.

Fig. 1. First draw a long straight line, and mark on it the length of BUST to measure. Starting from the bottom ; measure off for the slope of waist, the 2½ graduated inches required for the back neck, this will give the bottom of side seam, and from this point measure upwards the length of SIDE to measure. Draw lines square across at all the points, and mark on the bottom line half the length of WAIST to measure, *plus* 1½ graduated inches.

Fig. 2. Mark all the points indicated on this diagram, with a graduated measure cor-

(Plate 14.)

responding to the BREAST measure of the client, and complete the pattern by drawing the curves as before explained.

THE BACK, FIGS. 3 & 4.

Fig. 3. Draw a straight line, and mark on it the length of the CURVE to measure. Mark upwards from the bottom the length of SIDE to measure. Draw lines square across, and mark on the bottom line, 1½ graduated inches more than half the WAIST: this 1½ is an extra allowance given in the middle of back at the bottom only, and will afterwards be taken in by the strap and buckle, see fig. 8.

Fig. 4. Mark the other points of the back by the graduated measures, and complete it by drawing the curves, as shown on *Plate 13*.

The forepart and back drafted in this manner, will, in at least nine cases out of ten, fit perfectly well without any modification, except the lengthening below the natural waist, and other changes required by Fashion, for which see fig. 7.

If, however, the client differs very much

(Plate 14).

from the proportionate standard, and if a *very* perfect fit is required, the changes indicated on figs. 5 and 6 may have to be made.

FIG. 5.

If the client is *extremely* Extra-erect, or has an *extremely* round chest, give a little more round to the front edge, never more than ⅜, and take the same quantity away from the top of side seam, so as not to have the front too wide. This alteration will be but rarely required.

If the man is *very* Stooping, or has his chest unusually flat, take about ⅜ from the front of chest, and add it under the arm. Very flat chests are often met with, and this change should in most cases be made for them.

FIG. 6.

In most cases the SLOPE OF SHOULDER will be found correct, as it is drafted in fig. 4. In those cases however, where the shoulders are *extremely high* or *extremely low*, we may make the alterations indicated on this diagram, but seldom varying more than ¾ of an inch from the usual slope.

(Plate 14.)

The marks at A, B. in figs, 5 and 6, show how, by a judicious use of Fishes and Gussets at these places, the fit may be improved for the principal structures that vary from the proportionate.

For EXTRA-ERECT men, take out a small fish at A, and put in a small gusset at B.

For STOOPING men, put a gusset at A, and make a fish at B.

For VERY THIN WAISTS, take out a fish at A, leaving the front of waist a little wider to compensate for it.

For STOUT waists.   Put in a gusset at B, to allow for the fullness of the hips, and to prevent the back from working up, which it would do if it was too tight at this part.

It will now be seen, what a great degree of judgment is required in the use of Fishes, and Gussets, as if they were used in wrong places, they might completely spoil the fit.

The Forepart and Back, drafted like figs. 2 and 4, and corrected if required by figs. 5 and 6, are the wrapper or envelope of the body. It

(Plate 14.)

only descends a very little below the natural waist, and it buttons up from the top to bottom. It has now to be completed, or modified according to the particular style required ; giving it any of the forms indicated on *Plates* 15 and 16 ; or if the supplementary measures of Opening and Front length have been taken, we apply them directly to the draft, as shown by fig. 7.

HOW TO COMPLETE THE PATTERN.

Fig. 7, *Forepart.*   First mark upwards from the shoulder point, the width of back neck, and starting from this point, apply the measure of OPENING to fix the place of first button, and the bottom of crease line.   Starting again from the top, apply the measure of FRONT LENGTH, with $\frac{3}{4}$ of an inch added, to rule the bottom of waist: this $\frac{3}{4}$ is allowed for the shoulder seam, and the turning in at bottom.   The pattern can now be finished, by drawing the waist seam at its lengthened place, and shaping the shawl or the neck seam, to taste or to Fashion.   The pocket is usually about five inches long, and commences

DRAFT TO MEASURE.

14.

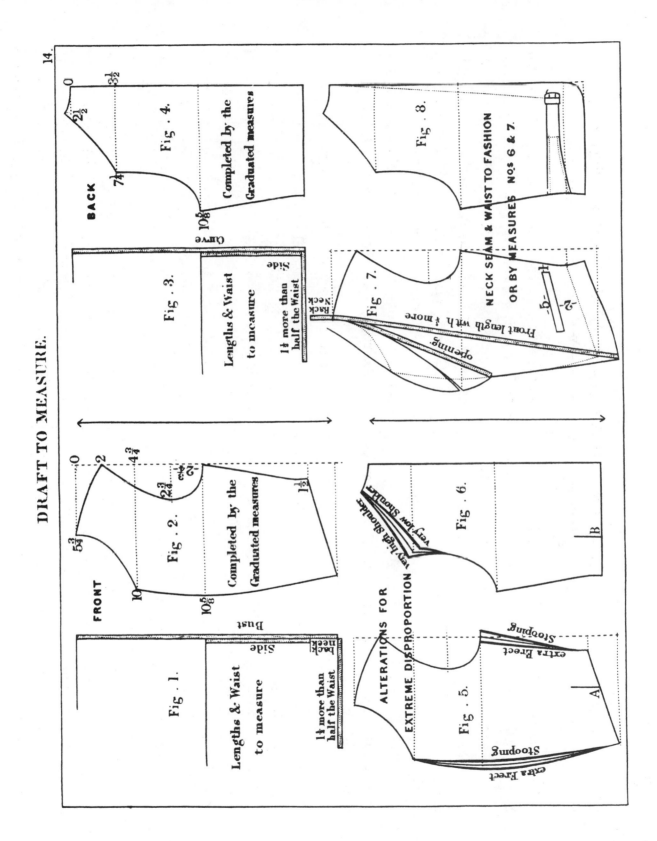

Fig. 4.

BACK

0 · 3½ · 2½ · 7¼ · 10⅝

Completed by the Graduated measures

Fig. 3.

Lengths & Waist to measure

1¼ more than half the Waist

Side

Curve

Fig. 8.

NECK SEAM & WAIST TO FASHION
OR BY MEASURES Nos 6 & 7.

Fig. 7.

Back Neck

Front length with ¼ more

opening

-2- -5-

Fig. 2.

FRONT

0 · 2 · 4¾ · 5¾ · 2¾ · 2¼ · 2½ · 10 · 10⅝ · 1½

Completed by the Graduated measures

Fig. 1.

Lengths & Waist to measure

1¼ more than half the Waist

Side

Back neck

Bust

Fig. 6.

very low Shoulder

very high Shoulder

B

Fig. 5.

ALTERATIONS FOR
EXTREME DISPROPORTION

extra Erect

Stooping

Stooping

extra Erect

A

(*Plate* 14.)

at 1 from the side seam, and is placed about 2 inches above the natural waist, as shown by the dotted line. There is nothing to be allowed at the front edge for the buttoning, as the necessary quantity is already given in the draft.

For the *Back* fig. 8, there is only to lengthen the waist to agree with that of the forepart. The straps commence at the side seams, and the edges are sewn to the back for about 4 inches, as shown on the diagram, the ends being left loose and a buckle added to one end, which is used to tighten in the 1⅜ inches, which are allowed in the middle of back beyond the measure; so that by letting out the strap, more ease may be given to this part if required.

CHANGES IN FASHION.

(*Plate* 15.)

The variations of form produced in Waistcoats by Changes of Fashion, are very numerous, but they may be reduced in practice to a small number of principal types, which are very easy to understand and to remember. In the backs

(*Plate* 15.)

there is (with one exception) no change whatever. We give the principal styles of Foreparts on *Plates* 15 and 16, which we will now proceed to explain.

Fig. 1. SINGLE BREASTED CLERICAL WAISTCOAT, buttoning up to the top, and having a narrow collar turned down all round. It will be seen that this is really nothing but the close fitting pattern, or wrapper of the body, lengthened at the waist as usual, to which is added a collar, cut in a similar manner to that of a coat, see Part 1.

On this diagram we have indicated the place of the tightening, which should in ALL our Waistcoats be given to the front edge. It should be tightened at the part indicated; a very slight degree will be sufficient, only just enough to bring the front edge nearly to a straight line: the fulness should then be pressed back, towards the prominent part of the chest. Where practicable, this manner of obtaining the roundness, is far preferable in most cases to taking out fishes or V's.

(*Plate* 15.)

Fig. 2. STRAIGHT FORM OF WAISTCOAT. This style is sloped off from the top button-hole, and has a narrow stand up collar. We have placed the opening at an average depth, but it may, of course, be made higher or lower than this, according to Fashion or to taste. If it is cut to open lower, the neck seam should of course be more sloped off : but the end of collar should not be placed lower than it is in this diagram.

Figs. 3 and 4. STRAIGHT FORM WITHOUT COLLAR. For this style, there are changes both to back and forepart. The back is raised up ⅜ at the neck, to supply the place of the collar ; at this, however, as will be seen by fig. 2, renders the shoulder seam of the back longer ; in order therefore to make that of the front equal to it, a small gusset must be put in the shoulder seam of the forepart, see fig. 3. The fronts may open higher or lower according to Fashion, or the wishes of the client : the most usual heights for the top button hole, are at 6¼ or 10¼, but this style may close nearly to the top, or it may

(*Plate* 15.)

open as low as fig. 2 in *Plate* 16. These limits of variation should never be exceeded.

Figs. 3 and 4 also show how the forepart may be made to take less stuff, by taking off any quantity (say 1 inch), from the side seam of forepart, and adding it to the side seam of back : the quantities added on and taken off, are shown by the dotted lines. When this alteration is made, care must be taken however to give room for the hip, by putting a small gusset at the bottom of back, so that the displacement of seam may not derange this part.

Fig. 5. DOUBLE-BREASTED LAPEL WAIST-COAT. This style, buttoning to the top, is often worn by Clerical Gentlemen. To obtain it we draft the close-fitting model type, and first take off all along the front edge, the ⅜ which has been allowed for the button holes in our model pattern : if this were not done, the seam would not be in the centre. The lapel and collar are cut exactly the same as for a frock coat, see Part 1, *Plates* 9 and 10, and pages 26 and 27. This style may have a turnover like a coat, if preferred.

VARIOUS STYLES

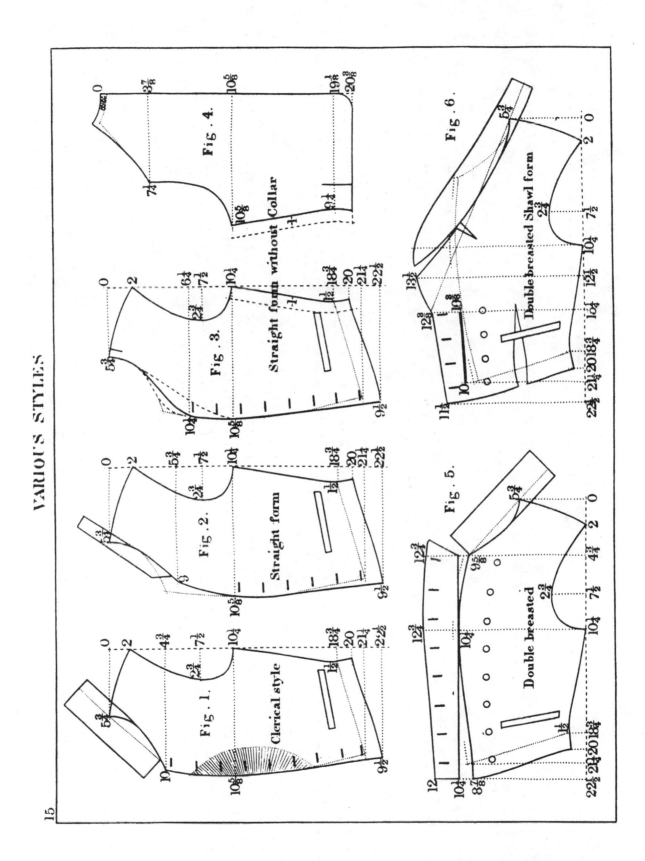

Fig. 1.

Clerical style

Fig. 2.

Straight form

Fig. 3.

Straight form without Collar

Fig. 4.

Fig. 5.

Double breasted

Fig. 6.

Double breasted Shawl form

15

(Plate 15.)

Fig. 6. Double-breasted Waistcoat with Collar of the Shawl Form. For this style, is first take off the ⅜ all along the front edge, the same as in fig. 5 ; the short dotted lines at the top, breast line, and the bottom, show the usual pattern, and the fine dotted line shows the corrected place of the front edge. Next take out a large fish in the waist seam to give the roundness for the chest, and in order to compensate for the fish, advance the bottom of waist as shown by the *strong black line,* which will form the centre of the double breast. Taking this line as a base, mark in front of it, about 2 inches at the top and 1½ at the bottom, for the front edge, and equal quantities on the other side of the line for the buttons. Next starting from just above the top button hole, draw a straight line touching the shoulder point ; this is called the *Crease Line.* Shape the shawl collar as shown on the diagram, or according to taste or Fashion, and take out a fish in the neck seam, to keep the edge of crease tight and assist the rolling back of the shawl.

(Plate 16.)

Fig. 1. Single-breasted Shawl Form, buttoning rather high. The cut of this style is very easy, if we take the close fitting pattern as a base. First mark the height of opening, and draw the crease line touching the shoulder point : then spring out beyond the dotted front edge, any quantity for the width of the shawl, according as the part which rolls over is required broader or narrower. At the top of crease line, mark on each side of it, the respective widths for the stand and fall of collar, and take out a small fish in the neck seam to assist the making up.

Fig. 2. Shawl Form, Opening Low. This style is cut in exactly the same manner as fig. 1, except that the opening is made much lower, so as to show more of the shirt front. A fish is taken out in the neck seam, and sometimes for this style another small fish is taken out in the waist seam, at the place marked by the dotted lines ; this is to assist in giving the roundness for the chest, as the front edge is of course too short for the fulness to be pressed back as in

(*Plate* 16).

other styles. This form of Waistcoat, is that generally worn for evening costume.

Fig. 3. SKIRTED WAISTCOAT. For this style a fish is made in the waist, the waist being widened at the bottom to compensate for it. A skirt about 4 inches deep is then added ; it is sloped off in front, and the back part has a seam made across as far as the fish ; this will give a better sit to the skirt on the hips. This style may be made either to button to the top, or it may be of the straight form with narrow stand up collar, as shown by the dotted line. It might even be of the shawl form like fig. 1. Skirted Waistcoats are now only worn for Livery, or for some Shooting or Hunting Costumes.

FISHES.

Figs. 4, 5, 6 and 7, explain the effects produced by taking out fishes in various parts of Waistcoats. A correct knowledge of these effects is of great importance to the Cutter, and will often enable him to adapt a Waistcoat perfectly, to those extremely disproportionate figures that are sometimes met with.

(*Plate* 16.)

The object of taking out fishes, is to give roundness to the chest : either because the chest of the client is unusually prominent, or because the material will not allow of the roundness being obtained in the usual way.

There are a great number of combinations for the position of these fishes, and many houses have their own special manner of taking them out. They may however, on examination, be reduced to four very simple cases, each of which requires a special compensation made for it in the cut of the forepart, so as not to derange the balance.

FISH IN THE SCYE.

Fig. 4. For Extremely Round Chests, it sometimes happens that the fulness given by the roundness of front edge is insufficient, or the material may be one that cannot be worked with the iron. In either of these cases a fish can be taken out in the Scye, which is compensated for by making the shoulder piece straighter, and also a trifle shorter, for the reason explained in Part 1, page 31.

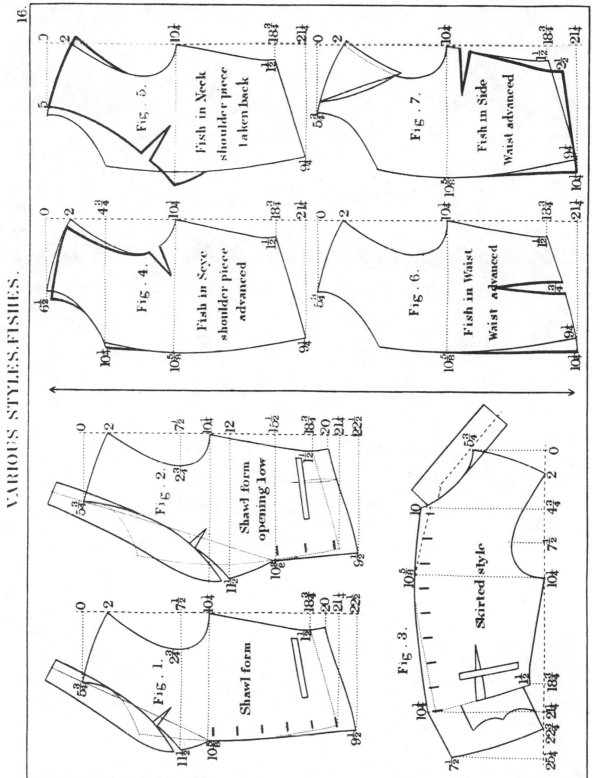

VARIOUS STYLES. FISHES.

Fig. 5. — Fish in Neck shoulder piece taken back

Fig. 4. — Fish in Seye shoulder piece advanced

Fig. 7. — Fish in Side Waist advanced

Fig. 6. — Fish in Waist Waist advanced

Fig. 2. — Shawl form opening low

Fig. 1. — Shawl form

Fig. 3. — Skirted style

16.

(Plate 16.)

This manner of taking out the fish is most suitable for Waistcoats of the Straight form, such as figs. 1, 2, or 3, *plate* 15.

FISH IN THE NECK SEAM.

Fig. 5. For Waistcoats of the shawl form, it will be remembered, a small fish is taken out in the neck seam, to give a better sit to the crease and to the shawl collar, and a small fish like this, does not affect the fit of the forepart. If however this fish is made larger, so as to give roundness to the chest, it must be allowed for by taking the shoulder piece back, as shown on this diagram.

In Waistcoats of the Shawl form where a large fish is required, it is generally taken out in the neck seam.

FISH IN THE WAIST SEAM.

Fig. 6. If it is preferred to have the front edge of Waistcoat nearly in a straight line, which is thought by many persons to be a better form to make up; this form may easily be obtained by advancing the front edge $\frac{3}{4}$ of an inch (or even more) at the bottom, graduating to no-

(Plate 16.)

thing at the breast line, and taking out a long fish in the middle of waist seam, as shown on this diagram.

For *Thin Waisted men,* that is for men having more than 3 inches difference between the breast and waist measures, we *always* recommend a fish being taken out in the waist, because the front edge would in these cases otherwise be-come too round. For Plaids, Stripes, or Checked materials, it is also better to take out a fish, and advance the waist so as to straighten the front edge ; because the line of the front edge, will then nearly correspond to the pattern on the material. This cut may be also used for any material which will not allow of being worked with the iron.

FISH IN THE SIDE SEAM.

Fig. 7. There are many cases in which, while it would be inconvenient to take out the fish as in fig. 6, it is nevertheless required to advance the waist. The pattern may be so strongly marked, that a fish taken out in the waist would become very conspicuous, and would destroy the

(*Plate 16.*)

effect of the material. In these cases we may take out the fish as in fig. 7, at the same time lowering the bottom of side seam, and advancing both the front edge and bottom of side. This cut has all the advantages explained for fig. 6, and is even better in many respects, because the fish under the arm is taken out exactly in the most suitable place, viz., opposite the prominent part of chest, and is besides in a position where it is never seen, and where consequently its interrupting the pattern is of no importance.

At the top of this diagram, fig. 7, we have shown how, by cutting off the corner of shoulder piece, and making a long fish, we can produce a better fit at this part, at the same time obtain *a great saving of material,* because the Forepart by this means, may often be cut out between the legs of a pair of Trowsers. Of course the corner piece must be made a trifle larger than the piece cut off, so as to allow for the loss produced by the seams

TROWSERS.

(*Plate 17.*)

The draft of Trowsers must be considered one of the most important parts of the art of Cutting. Success in this branch becomes very easy and simple, if we adopt true principles, but great difficulties will be met with, if the draft is based upon false ideas or ignorance of the human structure. A great deal has been written on this subject, and many systems have been proposed, most of which we have found more or less incorrect, and more calculated to perplex and to mislead, than to instruct.

The system which we give in this work, is based upon the results of careful study and long experience, and its correctness in practice has been fully tested, during many years and by innumerable experiments. We could name many houses both in London and in Paris, who have acquired a reputation for Trowsers cutting, and who owe their success entirely to the adoption of our System.

(Plate 17.)

The principal characteristic of well cut Trowsers are the following, and they are all combined in our System:—

1st. That when the wearer is standing up, the legs should naturally hang straight without forming creases, and the fork should fit cleanly and smoothly, the extra width which is required for sitting down and other movements, being allowed at the back: we can place it there, because this part being covered by the coat, a little extra fulness is of no importance. 2nd. That the wearer should be able to sit down, stoop, run, or in fact make any movement, without the Trowsers cutting him at the fork, and without the sit of the legs being much deranged. 3rd. That when the wearer is seated, the Legs of the Trowsers shall not drag up from the bottom, nor down at the waist. 4th. That the Trowsers should be of the proper height at the top of fly, or in other words that the slope of waist seam should vary according to structure. 5th. That the Trowsers should be cut in such a way, that with any amount of wear, the legs do not get much

(Plate 17.)

out of shape, and that the folds they form will be graceful. This result we have arrived at in our system, by the adoption of the PLUMB LINE.

This *Plumb line* must always be placed parallel to the edge of cloth, or in other words, must lay on the straight thread of the cloth, from top to bottom. If it is *not so placed*, the Trowsers will after a little wear, soon get out of shape, and will form very unsightly folds. The cause for this is;—that the straight thread of the cloth, not being laid on the Plumb line of the Trowsers, does not coincide with the Centre of Gravity, and consequently the legs must have a tendency to hang on the biais. The neglect of this most important point, is one of the greatest faults in the English systems of Trowsers Cutting.

We think we are justified in saying, that the Draft of Trowsers, which has hitherto been so little understood, as to he one of the most difficult and complicated parts of the Art of Cutting, is by our system reduced to such a few simple and self-acting rules, as to render it perhaps the easiest and most certain branch of the Art.

THE

PROPORTIONATE PATTERN.

(Plate 17.)

Fig. 1. We commence by giving the Model type, or proportionate pattern, which of course corresponds to the Coat in plate 2, and the Waistcoat in plate 13, and with them, forms a complete suit for a proportionate man. The style of this diagram is what is called the plain cut, and is the simplest form that can be given to a pair of Trowsers.

In order to examine in detail the various dimensions of this pattern, we must first mention that the line of construction from which the pattern is drafted, is the strong black line from 0 to 41½, which is called the Plumb line, and corresponds exactly in its position, to the measure called Front Length, which goes from the front of waist to the bottom of leg seam, and which shows the difference to make in height for Thin and Stout Waists.

The Lengths of the Trowsers are all reckoned in drafting, from the bottom of this Plumb line, and we find on examination—

First 31½, which is the length of leg seam in a proportionate man:—then 41 for the front of waist, which deducting the length of leg seam, 31½, gives 9¼ for the height of fall. Lastly there is 41½ for the height of the top of side seam, showing that the length of the side is rather more than that of the front, in the proportionate man. All these lengths are subject to considerable variation, according to the structure.

For the Widths; we find at the bottom, 8½ both for back and front, but they are only at this point for plain cut Trowsers.

On the fork line, we find outside, 9⅞ for the width of the pattern at the hip : on the inside we find 2 for the non-dress or right side of front, and 3⅛ for the left or dress side, which 3⅛ we may observe, is exactly one third of the width to the hip, 9⅞ : the fork point of back, is at 4¾ both for the right and left sides.

These points are fixed and invariable for all structures, when we draft by graduated measures,

(Plate 17.)

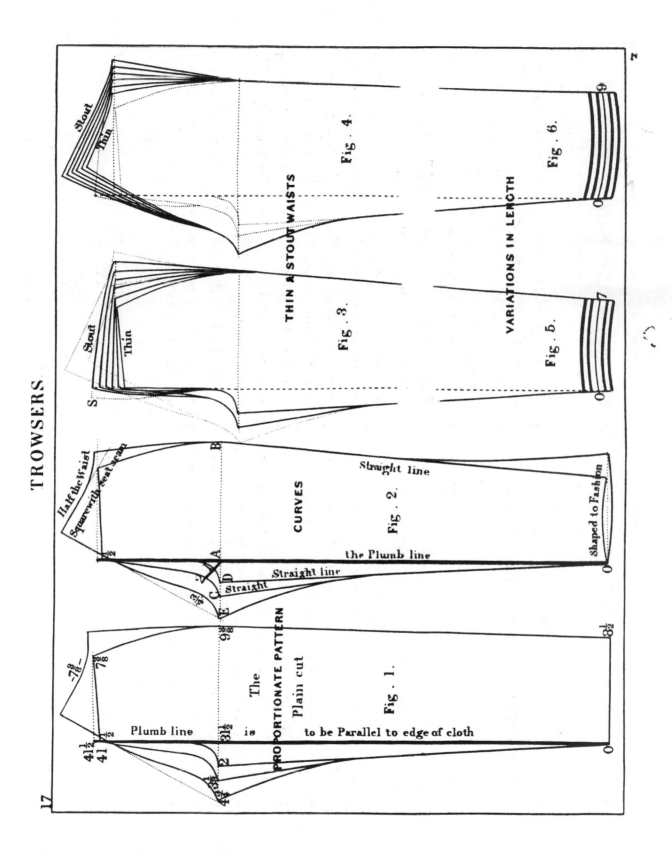

TROWSERS.

17

Fig. 1. — The PROPORTIONATE PATTERN Plain cut is to be Parallel to edge of cloth — Plumb line

Fig. 2. — CURVES — Half the Waist — Square with Seat seam — Straight line — the Plumb line — Straight line — Straight — Shaped to Fashion

Fig. 3. — THIN & STOUT WAISTS — Stout — Thin

Fig. 4. — Stout — Thin

Fig. 5. — VARIATIONS IN LENGTH

Fig. 6.

(Plate 17.)

At the waist we find; First, ½ inch for the slope of the seat seam of the back, measured along the top of waist from the plumb line; this degree of slope is fixed and invariable in drafting all Trowsers, and is measured, not on the dotted construction line, but along the waist seam itself. Second; the width of waist is 7⅞, or half the waist measure, 14¾: the other half of the waist (7⅞) is given to the top of back, starting from the top of seat seam as a base line.

A pattern for the proportionate structure is in Trowsers, not of so much service as it is in Coats and Waistcoats: it is only the figures on the fork line that are of great service, and all the lengths, as well as the size of waist, may vary in each different pair of Trowsers. For this reason, Trowsers are almost always made to measure.

THE OUTLINES, FIG. 2.

A correct knowledge of the exact form to be given to the various seams, is one of the most essential things in Trowsers Cutting. An error of ¼ inch in the place of a curve, or a single badly drawn line, may produce a very visible

(Plate 17.)

defect. We have therefore on fig. 2, given an explanation of all the straight lines and curves which form the Outline of the pattern, and this diagram should be studied with great attention.

THE TOP SIDE, OR FRONT.

The *Leg seam* is drawn in a *perfectly straight line*, from the *non-dress* point of the fork at D, to the bottom of plumb line at 0. If this Leg seam line were hollowed out, it would only be suited for bow legged men; if it were rounded it would only be suited for men whose knees touch each other, or nearly so. The line for the left or dress side of Leg seam, starts from point C, and goes in a straight line to join the line of the right side, at about ⅓ the length of leg seam.

For the *Hollow of the Fork*, measure diagonally from A (at an angle of 45 degrees, as shown by the black line), 1 for the curve of the right or non-dress side, and 1¾ or 2 for the left or dress side, and draw the curves through these points: the right side joins the Plumb line about 2½ above the dotted fork line at A; the left side joins it at the top.

H

(Plate 17.)

We have given no figures for the Bottom, because the dimensions vary according to Fashion.

The *Side seam* of front is drawn in a straight line from the bottom, to the outside of fork line at B: from B upwards it forms a slight curve to meet the side of waist.

The top or *Waist seam* is drawn in a perfectly straight line, except for very Stout Waists when it is a little rounded, see fig. 3.

THE UNDER SIDE, OR BACK.

For the *Seat seam*, draw a straight line from the outside point of fork at E, *always crossing the* WAIST SEAM *of the Front at* ½ *a graduated inch in*, from the Plumb line. The seat seam follows this line at the top, and for about one or two inches beyond the Plumb line. At the lower part, it is hollowed in ¾ of a graduated inch from the straight line, at about two inches above the fork. Some cutters hollow the seat seam more at this part, and others draw the seam with hardly any hollow at all: Extreme degrees however, either of straightness or hollowing out, may we think, produce defects.

(Plate 17.)

The upper part of *Leg seam* in the back, forms a very slight curve, and joins the leg seam of front, a little above the place where the dress and non-dress sides meet.

To mark the *correct Height* for the *Top of Back*, take the square, place it against the seat seam, and draw a line square from the seat seam, touching the side of waist of the front, as shown by the dotted line.* The *Waist Seam* of back follows this square line for about half the length, and then curves to about ¼ inch above the square line, which rules the height of side seam in the front. Make the length of this waist seam, equal to half the Waist measure, and from this point draw the side seam of back, to join the side of front at point B; from this point it follows the side seam of front, for about half the distance to the bottom, and then curves gradually outwards from this point, according to Fashion.

The bottom is of course shaped to Fashion.

* The top of back when drawn as thus described, is exactly at the Level of natural waist; many Cutters however prefer to cut this part of the Trowsers higher, and of course this may be done without in any way altering the fit of the Trowsers. In some cases it may indeed be an advantage to cut this part of the Trowsers higher, so as to give warmth to the loins.

(Plate 17.)

THE VARIOUS STRUCTURES.
(Plate 17).

On figs. 3, 4, 5, and 6, we have collected together examples of the principal Variations in Structure that are met with, and figs. 3 and 4 in particular, will we think be found of great service, in fixing the ideas as to the differences required to be made in the upper part of Trowsers, for the Thin and the Stout Waists.

A great deal of uncertainty and misapprehension prevails on this point, and very grave errors are constantly made. We have seen many pairs of Trowsers made for Stout men, which were absolutely unwearable, from having been cut too low at the top of fly, and we have remarked that most systems of Cutting take no notice of this point, or entirely overlook its real importance:

THIN & STOUT WAISTS. FIGS. 3 & 4.

Fig. 3. FRONT. It may be laid down as a principle, that for Thin Waists, the waist seam, instead of being drawn square with the Plumb line, requires sloping downwards at the front. For Medium Waists, it should be drawn square, and for Stout Waists this seam should slope upwards; more and more in proportion as the waist increases in size.

Let us take as an example, a young man of about twenty years old, having an extremely thin waist: he will require the top of waist sloping downwards. In a few years his waist will have become a little larger, and he will then require less slope; and in a year or so the waist must be drawn square with the Plumb line. As he becomes older, he will most likely become stouter at waist, and then the front of his Trowsers will require sloping upwards, and this slope will continue to increase in an almost regular proportion. In fact for a man of average size, we may even form a table for this slope, which will be tolerably accurate.

This table it must be observed, is only intended to fix the ideas, as to the gradual and proportionate increase which takes place in the height of top of fly, for stout men.

(Plate 17.)

Inches.

Waists of	14	or less, require a slope of	¾	downwards.
„	15	„ „	¼	„
„	16	„ „	¼	„
„	17	„ the waist drawn square.		
„	18	„ a slope of	¼	upwards.
„	19	„ „	½	„
„	20	„ „	¾	„
„	21	„ „	1	„
„	22	„ „	1¼	„
„	23	„ „	1½	„
„	24	„ „	1¾	„
„	25	„ „	2	„
„	26	„ „	2¼	„
„	27	„ „	2½	„

It will be seen by fig. 3, that for Stout Waists there is a difference in the curves of the Upper part of front. *First:* As the waist is Stouter, the side seam has less and less round given to it, and at last becomes quite straight. *Second:* For Stout men, the waist seam is cut rather round, instead of being straight. *Third:* The upper part of the fly seam, above the curve of the fork, should be cut rather rounded, instead of being drawn straight, as described for ordinary waists, fig. 2; both dress and non-dress sides, must of course rejoin the Plumb line at the top.

We have met with men having *extremely* and disproportionately large stomachs, who even required a little added on at the top of fly, as

(Plate 17.)

shown by the fine dotted line at S; but this change is hardly ever required, even in the most extensive practice.

Fig. 4. BACK. The Front being drawn as we have just described, according to the Size of Waist, the Back by our manner of drafting the seat seam, fig. 2, will become itself of the required form, without any trouble or calculation whatever. The top will become a little higher, and the extra width is distributed, about two-thirds at the side seam and the rest at the seat.

These two diagrams figs. 3 and 4, taken together, explain all the gradations that take place from very Thin to very Stout Waists.

VARIATIONS IN LENGTH.

Figs. 5 and 6. The changes caused by Variations in Length, are very simple, and merely consist in drawing the bottom lines higher or lower, as required by the measures.

MEASUREMENT. (Plate 18.)

Our system of Measurement for Trowsers, is very simple, and *Five Measures only* are re-

(Plate 18.)

quired, to indicate all the peculiarities of size, form, or structure : to which we may add Three Supplementary Measures, for the variations of shape caused by Fashion : see fig. 1.

The measures are taken by the common inch tape, and great care must be used to ensure accuracy. The measures should therefore, be taken deliberately, and without hurry.

PRINCIPAL SERIES.

No. 1. SIDE SEAM ; or length of side measured from the top to the bottom of the Trowsers, starting from the top of the side seam at the hollowest part of the waist, and *not* including the waistband. This measure should be taken tight, and it is the leg itself, not the Trowsers, which is to be measured.

No. 2. FRONT LENGTH, measured from the top of front, (*not* including the waistband), to the bottom of the inner leg seam. In Thin Waists, the measure will generally be less than the length of side seam : it will be longer for Stout men on account of the protuberance of the stomach, and by the difference it presents with

(Plate 17.)

the measure of *Side,* it indicates the proper degree of slope to be given to the front of waist. To take it correctly, the leg should be a trifle advanced as shown on fig. 1, and for Very Stout men, the measure should be kept close to the leg of trowsers, just below the fork.

N.B. Before taking the measures of *Side and Front,* it should first be noticed whether the Trowsers the client is wearing, are of the proper height at the waist. If they should happen to be either too high or too low, the measure must be taken from the *level of the Waist,* and not from the top of Trowsers. The waist of a pair of Trowsers should pass horizontally round the body, at the level of the natural waist of the man, and this level may be marked with chalk, at the top of side seam and top of fly, so as to form true starting points for these measures.

No. 3. LEG SEAM, taken in the usual way and with the greatest possible accuracy, as upon this depends the correctness of the length of the Trowsers. To take this measure, pass a pencil through the loop at the end of a Devere's measuring tape (see fig. 2 plate 4), and hold it close up in the fork of the Trowsers, letting the tape fall naturally to the foot at the bottom of leg seam. We may observe that when using the looped tape, it should not be pushed up too tight, or the leg seam measure would become

TROWSERS.—MEASUREMENT.

(Plate 18.)

too long, and the Trowsers would be too long in the legs.

No. 4. WAIST, measured in the usual way, underneath the waistcoat and rather tight : it will, for these reasons, be about 1 inch less than the waist measure taken for a coat, and in the proportionate man is $14\frac{3}{4}$ only.

No. 5. SEAT or HIPS, this is the size round the seat at the most prominent part, just over the hip joint. This measure often gives the same figures as the breast measure of the man, but is more frequently a little larger, and like that measure serves to indicate the graduated measure to be used when forming the draft for Trowsers. It is, like the waist, only to be written down as half, say $18\frac{3}{4}$ for a total of $37\frac{1}{2}$.

These measures when taken, may be written down in one line in regular order as follows :— Side, Front, Leg, Waist, Hips,—and for a proportionate man, will read thus :— $41\frac{1}{2}$, 41, $31\frac{1}{2}$, $14\frac{3}{4}$, $18\frac{3}{4}$.

SUPPLEMENTARY SERIES.

No. 6. *Thigh*, Taken as high up as possible.

(Plate 18.)

This measure indicates the allowances for Fashion, or the particular style required. In general it is the left or dress side which is measured.

N.B. The Thigh measure, when taken *tight* on the *dress* side, is usually equal to two thirds of the breast measure, say $12\frac{1}{2}$ for $18\frac{3}{4}$. When it varies from this proportion (which however very rarely happens) it indicates a variation in structure, which may be provided for as follows :— If the Thigh is *more* than two thirds the seat, make each of the fork points a trifle wider, say $\frac{1}{4}$ inch at most : if it is less than two thirds the seat, give a little *less* width to the fork points.

No. 7. *Knee*, taken according to Fashion : when it is for tight fitting Trowsers the knee must be bent.

No. 8. *Bottom*, also according to Fashion, or the style required.

DRAFT TO MEASURE.

We will now proceed to the explanation of the Draft to Measure, which is extremely simple and easy.

FIRST OPERATION, FIG. 2.

Draw first a long straight line, called the Plumb line, and starting from the bottom, mark on it the length of *Leg seam* to measure. Then starting also from the bottom, mark on this line

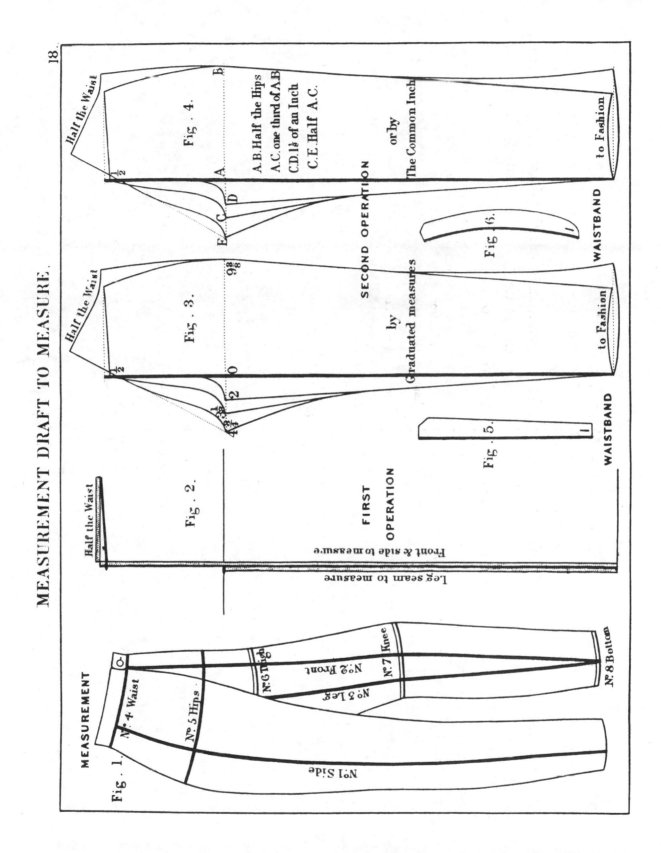

MEASUREMENT DRAFT TO MEASURE.

18.

MEASUREMENT

Fig. 1.

Nº 4 Waist
Nº 5 Hips
Nº 6 Thigh
Nº 2 Front
Nº 7 Knee
Nº 3 Leg
Nº 8 Bottom
Nº 1 Side

FIRST OPERATION

Leg seam to measure
Front & side to measure

Fig. 2.
Half the Waist

Fig. 3.
Half the Waist

$\frac{1}{2}$
0
2
9.8

to Fashion
WAISTBAND

Fig. 5.

SECOND OPERATION
by
Graduated measures

Fig. 4.
Half the Waist

$\frac{1}{2}$
A
D
C
E
B

A.B. Half the Hips
A.C. one third of A.B
C.D. 1¾ of an Inch
C.E. Half A.C.

or by
The Common Inch

to Fashion
WAISTBAND

Fig. 6.

to Fashion

(*Plate* 18.)

the lengths of *Front* and of *Side seam*; make a strong mark at the top of *Front length*, and at the height of *Side seam* draw a line square with the Plumb line, making this line the length of half the *Waist* measure. Draw the other lines square across at the fork and the bottom, and then draw the *Waist seam* from from the top of front to the top of Side seam, as shown by the black line.

SECOND OPERATION. FIG. 3 OR 4.

There are now two distinct ways of completing the draft. Some Cutters use the Common Inch measure only, and by it form the draft with divisions of the HIP or SEAT measure: this plan is shown on fig. 4.

Other Cutters simply use the Graduated Measures to mark the points, the *Seat* measure indicating the graduated measure to use: for instance;—if the client measures 18 at the Seat use the measure marked B. 18. If his Seat measure is 19½, use the measure marked B. 19½. and so on. The plan is, we must observe, far easier and more simple, and saves all calcula-

(*Plate* 18.)

tion and chance of error.

GRADUATED MEASURES USED.

Fig. 3. With a graduated measure, mark all the points on the fork line as on this diagram, for all sizes and structures; these points are:— 9⅜ for the outside width of front: 2 for the right point of fork, and 3⅛ for the left side: 4¾ for the fork point of the back.

Mark along the waist seam, from the top of *Front length*, ½ a graduated inch* from the plumb line, and draw the top of back and all the curves, as explained for fig. 2, *plate* 17.

COMMON INCH USED.

Fig. 4. If it is preferred to use the Common Inch only, we proceed as follows:—

Mark on the Fork line from A to B, half the Hip measure.

From A to C, one-third of this half, or one sixth of the Hip.

From C to D, 1⅛ common inches, taking care to add a little more than this for large sizes, and

* For Riding Trowsers a slope of 1 inch instead of ½ may be given, which will improve the fit for this purpose, and a fish may be taken out in the waist as explained for figs. 3 and 4, Plate 19.

(*Plate* 18.)

to make it a trifle less for small ones.

From C to E give half the width A C.

Slope in the seat seam $\frac{1}{2}$ an inch, on the waist line, and complete the pattern as usual. N.B. For very small sizes, only give $\frac{3}{8}$ slope to the seat, and for large sizes give $\frac{5}{8}$ or $\frac{3}{4}$ slope. Complete the pattern by drawing the outlines or curves.

We always ourselves prefer cutting out a pattern in paper, but many cutters prefer to draft at once upon the cloth. For this proceed as follows:—draw first the PLUMB LINE, *exactly parallel to the edge of cloth*, and form the draft of Front or top side. Cut this out, and then place it on the space intended for the back; being careful to lay the plumb line on the straight thread: the back can then be drafted as usual, in the easiest and most certain manner.

The Waistband we always prefer to cut separate. Fig. 5 shows the form for ordinary waists, and fig. 6 the form we recommend for very Thin Waists.

(*Plate* 19.)

Before proceeding to describe the various forms of Trowsers caused by changes in Fashion, we will take this opportunity of saying a few words on a modification (for we can scarcely call it a disproportion), of form that is sometimes met with. We refer to men who have the hips

(*Plate* 19.)

flat and the seat large. For these men the amount of round given to the hips on figs. 1 and 2, would be too much, whether in the small or large sizes: and it is therefore necessary to spring out the top part of the side seam of *under-side* and so reduce the round of the hip, and then to bring the waist back to its proper size, by taking out a fish just over the prominence of seat, as shown on figs. 3 and 4.

Figs. 1 and 2 are examples of draft by the Common Inch only, for a very small and a very large size.

Fig. 1. *Small size.* Waist measure $11\frac{1}{2}$, Hips $14\frac{1}{4}$.

We have on the fork line, $7\frac{1}{8}$ *outside*, or half $14\frac{1}{4}$. On the *inside*:—$2\frac{3}{8}$ for the left point of fork, or one-third of $7\frac{1}{8}$; for the right point $1\frac{3}{8}$, or 1 inch less than $2\frac{3}{8}$; for the back $3\frac{1}{2}$, or $2\frac{3}{8}$ *plus* $1\frac{1}{8}$ (which is nearly the half of $2\frac{3}{8}$).

Fig. 2. *Large size.* Waist 21, Hips 21.

On the fork line we find, first $10\frac{1}{2}$ outside, or half 21; then on the inside one-third of $10\frac{1}{2}$ (or $3\frac{1}{2}$) for the dress point of fork, and $1\frac{1}{4}$ less than

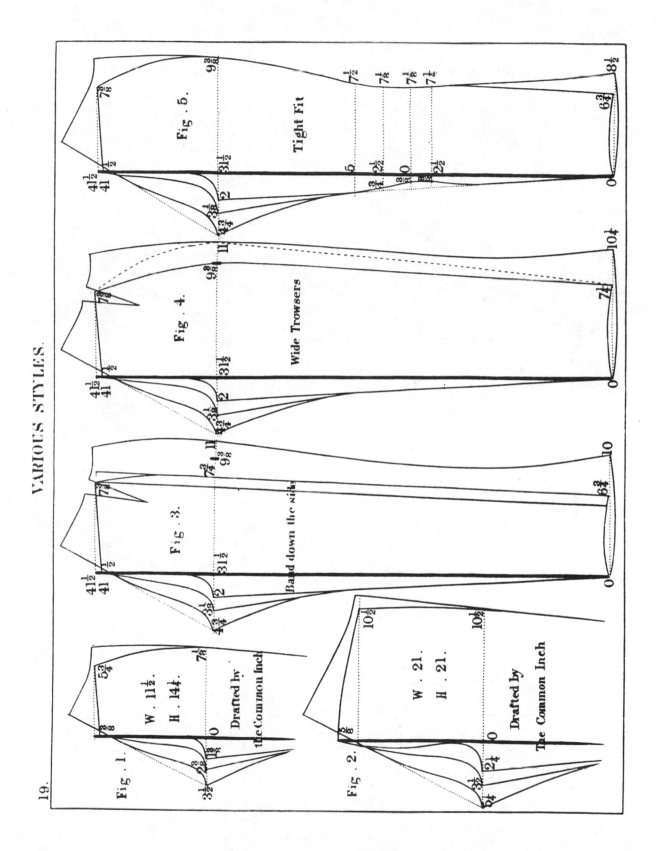

VARIOUS STYLES.

19.

Fig. 5.

Tight Fit

Fig. 4.

Wide Trowsers

Fig. 3.

Band down the side

Fig. 1.

W . 11½.
H . 14¼.

Drafted by
The Common Inch

Fig. 2.

W . 21.
H . 21.

Drafted by
The Common Inch

(Plate 19.)

this (2¼) for the non-dress point: the back fork is at 5¼, or 3½ inches with half of it (1½) added.

The waist is sloped upwards as before explained for stout men. In fig. 2 the slope of seat is at ⅜; in fig. 1 it is ⅝ only.

These two diagrams show at a glance how much better it is to use the graduated measures for the Draft of Trowsers; had we used them for these large and small sizes, instead of the common inch, the figures on the fork line and the slope of the seat, would have been exactly the same in both patterns, all the calculations and divisions of the hip measure would have been avoided, and much thought, time, and trouble would have been saved.

CHANGES IN FASHION.

As a general rule we may say, that changes in Fashion make no alteration in that part of the pattern, which is *inside* the plumb line: it is only the outside that is influenced by these alterations. These changes are very numerous, but we will however give a general idea of the

(Plate 19.)

principal styles, which will be oftenest required.

SIDE SEAM ADVANCED.

Fig. 3. This change, which is very often made, consists of taking a certain quantity from the side seam of front at the hip, and adding it to the back at the corresponding place. The side seam of front will then form an almost straight line, and this style, it will be at once seen, is exactly suited for materials having a band down the side. In the case of these banded materials, we cannot always draw the Plumb line parallel to the edge of cloth, but the degree of slope will be so trifling, as to be of slight importance. For this form, it is better to cut a fish in the waist of the under side, so as not to have the side seam of back too round.

WIDE TROWSERS.

Fig. 4. Instead of taking off from the front, what is added to the back; the front may remain at its usual place, and an *Extra width* be given to the back, so as to make the Trowsers wider at hips. This style is very often worn.

(Plate 19.)

TIGHT FITTING STYLE.

Fig. 5. This is merely the ordinary model type, drawn to measure, except that they are curved in at the knee to follow the form of the leg at this part. This is done as follows.

Mark for the bottom of knee-cap, at half the length of leg seam, and starting from this place measure on the Plumb line 2½ graduated inches upwards for the thickest part of knee, 5 upwards for the top of knee, and 2½ downwards for the top of calf; draw lines square across at these points. On the top line mark a width of 7½ outside. On the second line mark ¾ inside and 7⅞ outside. On the next line mark ⅜ inside and 7⅛ outside. On the bottom mark ⅜ or ½ inside and 7¼ outside, and draw the curves touching these points. The bottom to Fashion.

GAITER BOTTOM STYLE.

(Plate 20.)

Fig. 1. This style is, at the present time, not

(Plate 20.)

often required. It is obtained by adding at the bottom, any quantities to the back; say 1 inch inside, and 2 inches outside. It will be observed that the bottom of front is rounded, but it will be brought nearly straight in making up, by stretching the bottoms of leg and side seam. In the back, the bottom is cut hollow in the middle, and round at the side.

MAKING UP.

Many Tailors prefer to cut the Waistband in one piece with the Trowsers, by leaving an additional height of 1 or 1½ at the top, as shown by the strong black line at the top of fig. 1. Care must be taken however to spring out the top of side seams as indicated. We, however, much prefer to cut the Waistband separate, because it gives strength and firmness to the Trowsers at this part.

For *Trowsers worn without braces*, we recommend the plan shown at the top of fig. 2, which is:—Cut the front as usual *without* the Waistband, and the back with the waistband on it, as shown by the strong black line, taking out a

(Plate 20.)

small fish to give a closer fit at this part. A Waistband is then cut out as usual, and joined on to the front: it is stitched over the waistband of back as far as the fish, and the ends are then left loose, one forming a strap, and the other having a buckle attached, so that the Trowsers may be tightened in as required.

On the lower part of fig. 2, we have shown the way in which the leg and side seams must be made up, especially in the closer fitting styles of Trowsers, so as to obtain the proper shape for the knee and for the calf. For about 5 inches above the line representing the lower part of the knee, stretch the backs a little, both at leg and side seams, and full in the fronts. Below the knee, for about from 5 to 8 inches, stretch the fronts and full in the backs.

The quantities of stretching and fulling, vary according to the material, or as the Trowsers are loose at the knee like fig. 4, *plate* 19, or Tight fitting, like fig. 5 in the same plate. Wide Trowsers may be made up fair, Plain Cut Trowsers require hardly any stretching or full-

(Plate 20.)

ing at all, while Tight fitting Trowsers may have as much as half an inch. To ensure the workman giving the proper degrees of stretching and fulness, it is the best plan to make marks at the leg and side seams both in front and back, as follows, fig. 2:—Draw first a line square across at the height of half the leg seam, and then draw two other lines square across, one 5 inches above, and the other from 5 to 8 inches below it. At the top and bottom lines, make chalk marks on the side and leg seams both of back and front. At the place of the middle line, make a mark at each side of the *front* only, and for the back, make chalk marks a little higher up than the line. In making up, these chalk marks must be brought opposite to each other. The Leg Seam of *Underside* should be a little fulled just below the fork point $4\frac{3}{4}$, or if preferred, this fork point may be cut a little lower than the fork line, so as to make this part equal in length to the *Top side.*

We have several times said that the Plumb line should be drawn parallel to the edge of

(Plate 20.)

cloth, and we will now give an additional reason for this manner of placing it. When the Plumb line goes by the straight thread of the cloth, the leg and side seams have both nearly the same biais or slope, and consequently when made up, if these seams stretch at all, they will do so equally on both sides, and the balance or way in which the legs hang, will not be deranged. But if, as is often done to save material, the *Side Seam* is placed at the edge of the cloth, then this seam being on the straight thread, will not stretch at all, but the leg seam being much on the biais, may stretch considerably; thus causing this part to be too long, deranging the balance, and causing the legs to form bad folds and hang ungracefully.

BREECHES.

Breeches are cut in a similar manner to Trowsers, and the measures taken are the same, except that instead of going to the boot, the Lengths are only measured down to a garter, fastened about 1½ inches below the knee.

(Plate 20).

Fig. 3. DRESS BREECHES. Also worn by Footmen. These are drafted exactly in the same way as trowsers, except that they only reach to 1½ below the knee, so that all the lengths are about 14¼ shorter. At the bottom the front is cut round and should be a little fulled, so as to give room for the knee cap : the back is cut hollow, and should be a little stretched.

Fig. 4. LOOSE BREECHES ; worn for Livery by grooms, gamekeepers, and others. These are drafted in the same way as fig. 3, except that an extra length (say 2½) is added at the bottom, so that the breeches may form creases crosswise, just above the knee. Besides this, the side seam is cut with extra width at the hips so as to fit easy ; and at the bottom the front is cut narrower, and the back wider, so as to make the buttons come more forward, in order to range with the buttons of the gaiter.

KNICKERBOCKERS.

These are in reality very wide Trowsers, made rather short, and fulled into a band at the bottom, which is fastened just below the knee, the

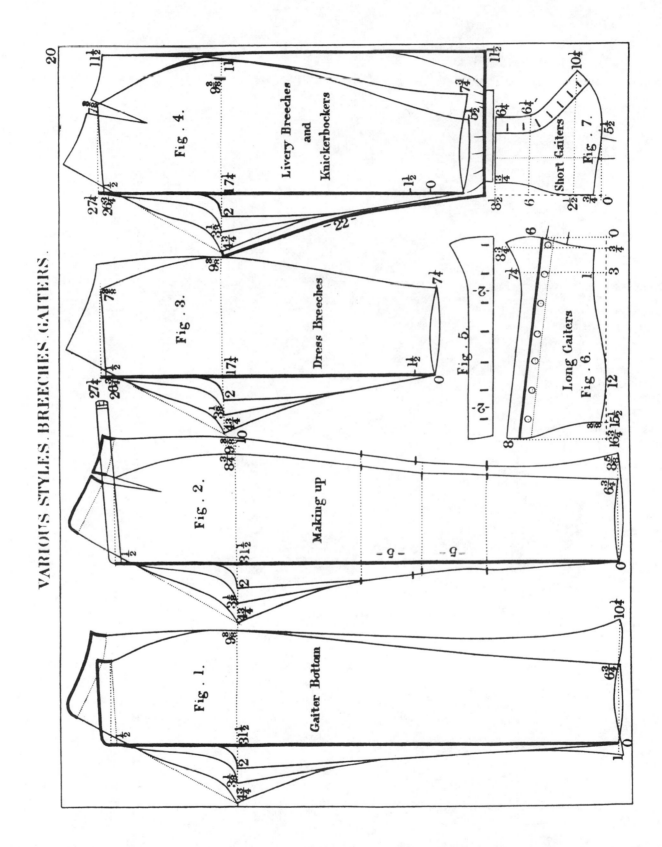

VARIOUS STYLES. BREECHES. GAITERS.

Fig. 4.

Livery Breeches
and
Knickerbockers

Fig. 7.

Short Gaiters

Fig. 3.

Dress Breeches

Fig. 5.

Long Gaiters

Fig. 6.

Fig. 2.

Making up

Fig. 1.

Gaiter Bottom

(*Plate* 20.)

legs falling over in graceful folds. These elegant garments are worn by the Rifle Volunteers, and also for Shooting or Deer Stalking Costumes. They are cut as shown by fig. 4, taking the black lines for the leg, bottom, and side seams. The measures should be taken as for Breeches, to about 1½ below the knee, and 4½ or 5 inches *extra length* should be allowed below 0, so as to make the leg seam about 22 inches long. The width at the bottom is 11½, and the side seams above this point are drawn parallel to the plumb line, so that the width at top is also 11½ inches. The upper part of the pattern is drafted in the same way as for Trowsers, except that a little extra width, say ¾ inch, may be given to the fork point of the back only. The size of the band or garter, must of course be ruled to measure: it may fasten either by a button, or a strap and buckle.

GAITERS.

Long Gaiters, figs. 5 and 6. We have here given the most improved pattern of Long gaiters or Leggings. It is the form generally adopted

by the various Rifle Corps for their Leggings, and then made in leather. The pattern is composed of three pieces. *First*, the whole side, cut like the outside plain line of fig. 6. *Second*, the button side, cut like the back part of fig. 6, as far as the strong black line. *Third*, the strap for the button holes, shown on fig. 5, and cut like the front part of fig. 6, as far as the dotted line. If preferred, the strap for the button-holes may be cut 3 inches wide instead of 2 inches, so as to make the buttons come more backward. The button side of leg need not then be cut so wide. For Livery Gaiters, see "*Devere's Modern British Liveries.*"

Short Gaiters, fig. 7. These may be made to fasten at the front, as shown on this diagram, but they are now more generally made to fasten at the sides, as shown by the dotted line; the strap and buttons at the fronts being added as ornaments only.

Both Long and Short Gaiters are to be drafted by the graduated measures, selecting a larger or smaller measure, according to the size required.

UNIFORMS.

(Plate 21.)

Military Uniforms may be said to form almost a special branch of the trade, and the making of these garments is confined to a comparatively small number of houses. We do not therefore, think it necessary to enter into *all* the very minute details of the Department.

We have given on *plate* 21, exact patterns of the Dress Tunic, and Undress Patrol Jacket, worn by the Infantry Officers of the British Army, and we have marked with great exactness, all the various dimensions of these patterns, as well as the ornaments on sleeves and collars, the buttons, and other details, according to the latest Government Regulations.

After describing these patterns, we will name the chief differences to be made in the form of Uniforms, for other parts of the Army, such as the Cavalry and the Rifle Brigade, and will add a few words on the styles generally adopted by the Volunteer Rifle Corps.

For all minor details respecting Uniforms, we

(Plate 21.)

beg to refer our readers to the Government Handbook, called "Regulations for the Dress of Officers of the Army." For the patterns of the various laces, badges, braiding, &c., which are very numerous, our readers must refer to any Army Lace and Accoutrement Manufacturer.

MANNER OF DRAFTING.

Uniforms are of course to be cut on the same principles, as those we have already described for coats. The measures are to be taken in the same manner, and the close-fitting pattern is to be drafted to measure in the square, as described in Part 1. This being done there must be a few alterations made, to suit the particular style required in a Uniform, and which we will now explain.

In the Tunic Back, fig. 2, there is no change, except that it is cut a little wider at the back stretch, narrower at waist, and is lengthened about 1¼ inch: it is placed at the edge of square, there being no seam in the middle.

For the Tunic Forepart, fig. 1. The front of neck is raised up 1 inch ; the shoulder piece is

(Plate 21.)

straightened $\frac{3}{4}$, because in a Uniform there is no fish taken out in the neck seam. The scye point of shoulder seam is also a little raised, because when the shoulder piece is straightened, there must be a less degree of stretching given to the front of scye. The waist is lengthened nearly $\frac{3}{4}$ at front, and about $1\frac{1}{4}$ at back: it is lengthened this quantity at back, so that the back buttons may come below the Waist belt. As the waist of a Uniform is always cut tight, a fish is taken out under the arm, instead of springing out for the hips.

The Hind Arm seam of the Sleeve is, in Uniforms, usually pitched at the bottom of Back scye, and many tailors obtain this effect by cutting the back scye $\frac{1}{2}$ an inch higher, as shown on Plate 8, fig. 3; at the same time widening the back neck, and deducting equal quantities from the shoulder piece. We however think that this antiquated style has an extremely ungraceful appearance, and we prefer to leave the back scye at its regular place, and (if thought necessary) to alter the position of hind arm seam

(Plate 21.)

of the sleeve at the top, as shown by the dotted lines on fig. 9, adding on half an inch to the top side, and taking the same quantity from the under side, at the corresponding place.

FULL DRESS TUNIC. FIGS. 1 TO 6.

This form is that worn by OFFICERS of THE LINE, and the MILITIA. It is made of scarlet cloth, with edgings of white cloth $\frac{1}{4}$-inch wide, at the front of foreparts and skirts, top and front of collar, and back pleats.

The *Forepart*, fig. 1, is Single breasted, and has a ketch cut on the right forepart, as shown by the dotted line, so as to button well over. There are eight regimental buttons up the fronts, and we may observe that the ends of button holes should be about $\frac{3}{4}$ an inch from the edging of front, so that the buttons may not overhang. At the waist seam, near the centre, a large hook is placed, to support the waist belt. On the left shoulder only, is a double strap of square gold cord fastened to a button near the neck, and serving to keep the sash in its place.

The *Collar*, is a little less than 2 inches deep, with front corner rounded off: it is made of cloth of the color of the Regimental Facings, which varies in almost every regiment. The badges on it denote the rank of the Officers, as described hereafter; that of fig. 1, is called a "Star," the badge on fig. 6, is a "Crown."
N.B. The lace on Uniforms and also the buttons, are of gold for the Army, silver for the Militia.

The *Back*, fig. 2, is $1\frac{1}{4}$ wide at waist, so that the hip buttons may be 3 inches apart. The pleats are edged with white.

The *Skirt*, fig. 3, is of moderate fulness, and $10\frac{1}{2}$ inches deep for a man of 5 feet 9 inches high: it may be made $\frac{1}{4}$ inch longer or shorter, for every inch difference in height from this standard.

The *Sleeve*, is cut like fig. 9, but for the Tunic it has a pointed cuff of the color of the Regimental facings, laced according to the following regulations for Distinction of rank.

(Plate 21.)

DISTINCTIONS OF RANK.

SLEEVES.

ENSIGNS AND LIEUTENANTS. FIG. 4.

The pointed Cuff is laced at the top with one row of half inch regimental lace, up to a point, 7½ inches in height, and is traced *outside* with gold Russia braid, finishing with an Austrian knot at top, making it 9½ high, and showing a light of 3-16ths of an inch of scarlet cloth between the lace and the braid. Traced inside with gold Russia braid, finishing down the cuffs with a 'crow's-foot" and eye, and showing a light of 3-16ths of an inch of the facing cloth between the bottom-edge of the lace and this braid.

CAPTAINS. FIG. 5.

The Cuff to have two rows of lace, showing a quarter of an inch light of the facing cloth between the two, and also between the bottom-edge of the lower lace and the braid; the top of the upper lace coming in a point 8 inches high, traced and finished at top and bottom of the gold lace, as described for ensigns and lieutenants, the top tracing and knot extending 10 inches high.

MAJORS. FIG. 5.

The same as for captains, with the addition of eyes to the *top* row of braiding above the upper lace, and showing 3-16ths of *scarlet* cloth between the lace and the eyes.

COLONELS AND LIEUTENANT-COLONELS. FIG. 5.

The same as for majors, but with eyes to the braid *under* the bottom lace, and showing 3-16ths of the *facing* cloth between the lace and the eyes.

COLLAR.

CAPTAINS, LIEUTENANTS, AND ENSIGNS. FIG. 1.

Color of the regimental facing, laced round the top with regimental lace and having the collar-seam covered with gold braid,

FIELD OFFICERS.

A row of gold braided eyes below the lace, in addition to the lace and braid; see fig. 6.

Relative badges for collars as before :—

Colonel, a Crown and Star. *Lieut. Col.* a Crown   *Major,* a Star.
Captain, a Crown and star.   *Lieut.* a Crown.   *Ensign,* a Star.

(Plate 21.)

The Shoulder Sash is flat and composed of 3 stripes of gold lace and 2 stripes of crimson silk half an inch in width, placed alternately, thus making the whole width of the sash 2½ inches; the two ends are passed through a slide of gold and crimson plait, and on each end is a rich flat tassel of crimson and gold 9-in. long.

Trowsers, blue cloth for Summer, Oxford mixed for Winter, with a ¼-inch scarlet welt at the side seams. For Full dress or State occasions, the side seams of the Trowsers are trimmed with two bands of ⅜ inch gold lace, with a ¼ inch stripe of crimson between them.

PATROL JACKET, FIGS: 7 TO 9.

The *Patrol Jacket,* (figs. 7, 8 and 9) is made of dark blue cloth, and is trimmed all round by black Mohair braid, one inch wide, which is also carried up the slits or openings which are left at the bottoms of seam under the arm (fig. 7.) The fronts fasten by hooks and eyes, and have one row of knitted Olivets up the fronts at equal distances, accompanied by four double drop loops of ¼-inch flat plait braid, with double eyes in the centre; the top loop 8¼ inches long, and the bottom loop 6 inches. Austrian knot on sleeve for all ranks, measuring 7 inches from the bottom of sleeve to the top of knot (fig. 9.) At the back, a braiding of ¼-inch flat plait, is placed just above the curved side seams, forming crows' toes at top and bottom, and having two pairs of eyes at equal distances; the eyes to be about 1 inch apart at waist, measuring from edge to edge only. Stand-up collar, with braid on top edge only. Pockets in front skirts, with flaps to turn in or out; *inside* breast pocket on the left side as shown by the dotted line.

When made up, the length of back (not including the collar) is to be 28 inches, for a man 5-ft. 9-in. in height, and ¼ an inch longer or shorter, for each inch of difference in height from the standard of 5-ft. 9-in.

There are no badges on the collar, except for field Officers, who have their distinctive badges embroidered *in gold.*

We may observe that the sword-belt is worn *underneath* the Patrol Jacket; and that the shoulder sash is *not to be worn in undress.*

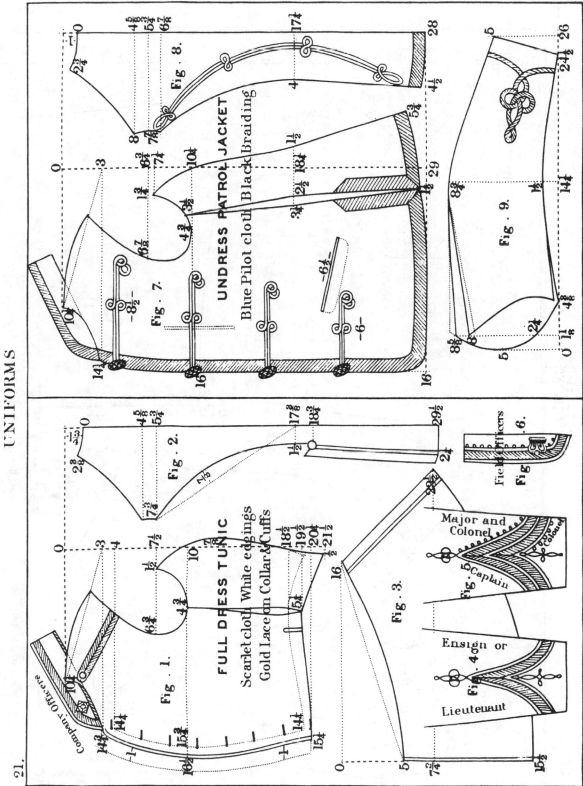

UNDRESS PATROL JACKET

Blue Pilot cloth Black Braiding

Fig. 7.

Fig. 8.

Fig. 9.

FULL DRESS TUNIC

Scarlet cloth White edgings
Gold Lace on Collar&Cuffs

Fig. 1.

Fig. 2.

Fig. 3.

Company Officer

Field Officers
Fig. 6.

Major and Colonel
Fig. 5. Captain

Ensign or
Fig. 4. Lieutenant

21.

This plate is from the first edition, see Introductory Notes.

UNIFORMS

21.

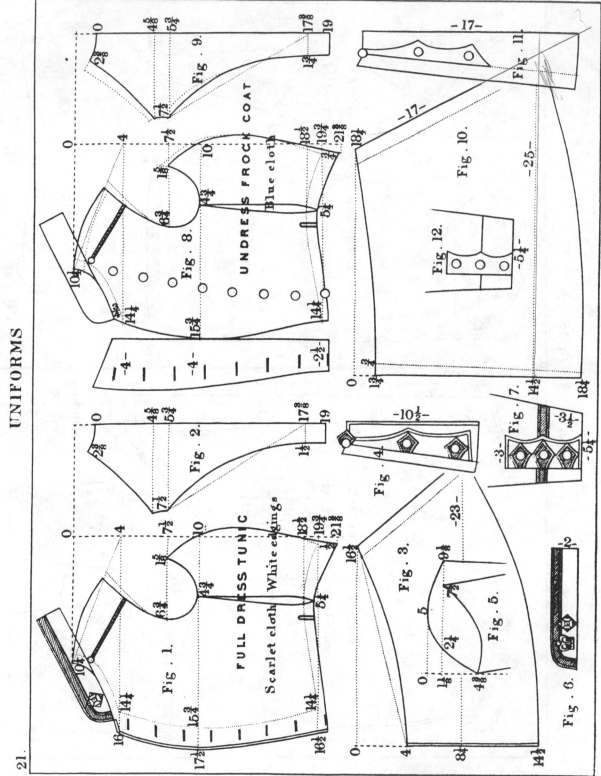

Fig. 9.

Fig. 8.

UNDRESS FROCK COAT
Blue cloth

Fig. 11.

Fig. 10.

Fig. 12.

Fig. 2.

Fig. 1.

FULL DRESS TUNIC
Scarlet cloth   White edgings

Fig. 4.

Fig. 7.

Fig. 3.

Fig. 5.

Fig. 6.

(Plate 21.)

For the CAVALRY, the form of the *Dress Tunic* is nearly the same, except that the skirt is only 9 inches in depth. The *Frock Coat* is single breasted without lapel, fastening by hooks and eyes, and ornamented by four rows of olivets and loops of thick braid.

The RIFLE REGIMENTS, have a Dark Green *Tunic*, single breasted, closing by hooks and eyes, with 5 loops and olivets at front; the skirts 9 inches deep. The *Undress* or Patrol Jacket, is of the same form as figs. 7 and 8, and is trimmed with *flat* braid.

The Uniforms of the VOLUNTEER RIFLE CORPS, are so numerous and varied, that they might almost form the subject of a special study. As a general rule however, we may say :—

The Grey Uniforms, are cut like figs. 1 to 7 ; the pointed cuffs being generally worn much smaller, and the sleeves richly embroidered in silver for the Officers.

The dark Green Uniforms, are either similar to the dress Tunic of the Rifle Brigade, or are of the same form as the Patrol Jacket.

(Plate 21.)

MAKING UP.

For the Infantry, the DRESS TUNIC skirt is lined with white. The pockets are placed inside at the back plaits. A small cash pocket is sometimes placed in the waist seam, and a watch pocket on the left breast, near the fifth buttonhole from the top. The body of the Uniform Tunic is moderately wadded, and lined with drab serge, which is usually quilted in diamonds. A leather band should be sewn round the waist inside, to prevent stretching.

The PATROL JACKET is lined with black serge, the body being lightly wadded and quilted.

As great exactness is required in the fit, Uniforms should always be tried on : it is a very good plan *always* to leave about ½ an inch extra stuff, all round the neck and at the top of back, and mark with the chalk when trying, the exact place at which the neck seam should be, as this is an important thing in a Uniform.

A Uniform Coat we may observe, generally requires to be cut more erect than an ordinary coat for the same man.

LADIES' RIDING HABITS.
(Plate 22.)

Figs. 1 and 2, show the proportionate pattern or wrapper of the body. It should be taken for the size required, by using a graduated measure, and when drafted by a measure marked B. 17¼, is for a Lady of proportionate or average size and structure, whose measures are:—breast 17¼, waist 13½, length of back 16¼.

Strictly speaking, this pattern, like the back and forepart of a coat, has certain points which are invariable for all structures and sizes, and others which should be varied in each pattern, by the application of the measures. It will however be found in practice that Ladies who take Equestrian exercise, do not as a general rule, deviate much from the proportionate standard, and the chief differences are these:—
The Breast measure may be larger or smaller.
The Waist may be thinner or stouter than the proportionate, as compared with the Breast.
The Length of Back, compared with the Breast measure, may be more or less than the standard.

(Plate 22.)

These differences may in general be provided for as follows:—

Draft the pattern according to figs. 1 and 2, by a graduated measure nearest the *Breast* measure of the lady. Apply the *Waist* measure to the pattern, and increase or diminish the size of the fishes, if the waist is too large or too small. Apply the *Length of back*, and shorten or lengthen the pattern, if required.

This will in most cases, produce a good fitting pattern, but if a more exact method is preferred, the Habit may be drafted to measure.

MEASUREMENT.

The measures to be taken, are only 5 in number. *Breast* : taken under the arms, round the largest part of the body. *Waist* : taken rather tight. *Curve and Bust* : both taken as described for coats, from the middle of back neck, to a centre point marked at two-fifths of the waist. *Side* : taken with the looped tape and pencil.

DRAFT TO MEASURE.

Figs. 3 and 4 show the manner of drafting a Habit to measure. It will be observed that on

(*Plate 22.*)

both these diagrams, there are 3 lines for the lengths—the construction lines, and two shaded bands by the side of them: in reality each diagram ought to have all the lengths marked on the construction line, but we have placed them here side by side, to render them more distinct, and to avoid confusion between the lengths.

In drafting a Habit; first draw two parallel lines about 10 or 11 inches apart, which form the construction lines of back and forepart· Draw a line square across at the bottom, for the bottom of back and the hollow of the hip.

THE BACK. FIG. 4.

Lengths. Mark the length at $1\frac{1}{4}$ less than the Curve measure. Mark for the depth of bottom of back scye, one-third of the length, *plus* $1\frac{1}{4}$. Mark above this, $2\frac{1}{4}$ graduated inches for the top of back scye. Draw lines square across.

Widths. With a graduated measure, mark the width of back neck $2\frac{1}{2}$: the top and bottom of back scye respectively at 9 and 8, and the width of waist at $1\frac{1}{2}$. Rise up $\frac{1}{2}$ for the curve of back neck, and draw the curves as fig. 4.

(*Plate 22.*)

THE FOREPART. FIG. 3.

Lengths. First continue the square line, at the bottom of back scye, into the compartment for the forepart; this gives the height of side point. Then starting from the level of the bottom or hollow of the hip, mark upwards the length of *Bust* to measure, less the back neck: this gives the top of front. Then starting also from the same point on the hip, mark upwards the length of *Side* measure, for the depth of scye.

Mark below the scye, $2\frac{1}{4}$ graduated inches for the height for the top of fishes. Starting from the top of construction line at 0, mark downwards $3\frac{1}{4}$ and $4\frac{1}{2}$, for the neck point and the slope of shoulder, Mark below the bottom line, $1\frac{1}{8}$ for the bottom of front edge and the points of fishes, and $\frac{3}{8}$ below, for the bottom of side.

Widths. Mark with the Graduated Measure:—11 for the shoulder point; $14\frac{1}{2}$ for the neck point or top of front edge; 2 and $6\frac{1}{4}$, for the side point and front of scye; $4\frac{1}{4}$ and $15\frac{3}{4}$, for the bottom of scye and the width of chest; 10 and $11\frac{3}{4}$, for the tops of the two fishes; 5 for

(Plate 22.)

the hollow of the hips, and 11¾, 12¾ for the width of strap between the fishes ; 17½ for the front of waist ; and ¾ for the taking in of the bottom of side : the size of the fishes at waist, is regulated by the difference between the Breast and the Waist measures ; half this difference being marked from 12¾ to D, and half from 11¾ to W : so that for instance, if a lady measures 5 inches less at Waist than at Breast, each fish will be 2¼ inches wide, and so on.

CHANGES IN FASHION.

The pattern as drafted from figs. 1 and 2, or to measure like figs. 3 and 4, is the simplest form that is given to a Habit. The fronts are meant to fasten by hooks and eyes, from the neck to the waist, and the waist seam is about at the place of the natural waist. For other styles, alterations must be made, in the same manner as described for Coats and Waistcoats.

If the Habit is intended to fasten by *Buttons*, about an inch extra must be added at the front edge : there may be a collar and turnover similar to a coat, as shown by the black line on fig. 3,

(Plate 22.)

or there might be a collar of the shawl form.

The Habit may be made *Pointed at back and front*, by lengthening the waist as shown on figs. 3 and 4, graduating to nothing at the hip.

Another style of Habit, which is often required, has a skirt cut in one piece with the body, as shown by the dotted lines at the bottom of figs. 3 and 4. The back, side body, and forepart, are all lengthened, and considerably sprung out at the bottom, so as to give room for the prominence of the hips.

The Sleeve. Fig. 5 is the close fitting sleeve, to be drafted by the graduated measures, ruling the length to measure. It may be made wider at elbow or wrist, as explained for coats.

The Small Skirts, sometimes called jacket skirts, are cut like figs. 6 or 7. In fig. 6, the back plait is the line 0, 11½, and the front edge is from 5¼ to 13¾, if the fronts are intended to meet ; if they are to be cut away from the waist, take the line 5¼ 12⅛. It may be made longer or shorter, if preferred, adding on or taking off any quantity equally all round the bottom.

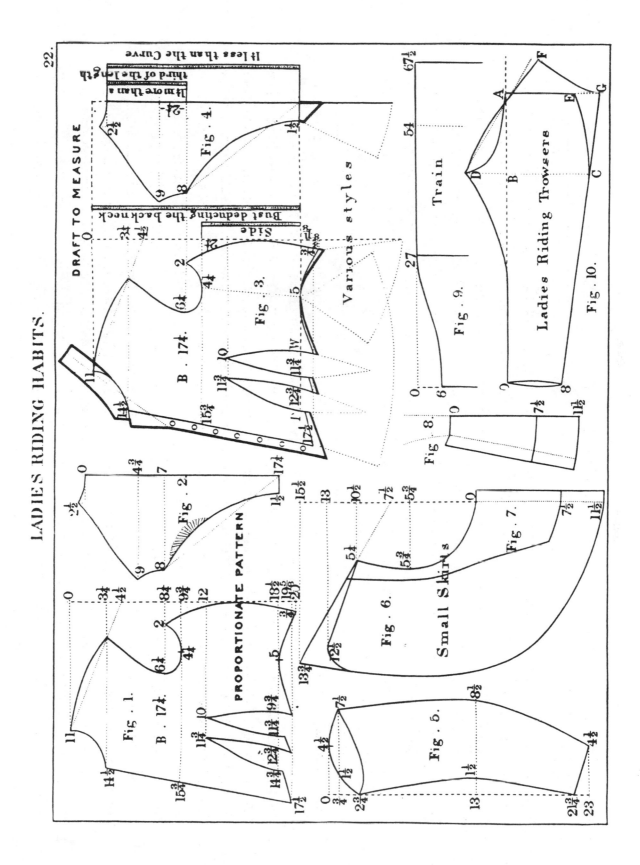

LADIES RIDING HABITS.

22.

DRAFT TO MEASURE

If less than the Curve

If more than a
third of the length

Bust deducting the back neck

Fig. 4.

Side

Fig. 3.

Various styles

Fig. 1.

B. 17¼.

PROPORTIONATE PATTERN

Fig. 2.

Fig. 6.

Small Skirts

Fig. 7.

Fig. 5.

Train

Fig. 9.

Fig. 8.

Ladies Riding Trowsers

Fig. 10.

(Plate 22.)

Fig. 7 is the Postillion skirt, very narrow at front and sides, and of a moderate length at back

Fig. 8 is the *back skirt*: the length must be ruled according to that of back part of front skirt.

THE TRAIN.

Fig. 9 is the Train or long skirt, reduced to a small scale so as to occupy less room on the plate. It consists of 2½ breadths of cloth. The breadth, which is sloped off 6 inches in front, line from 6 downwards, is the fold of the first graduating to nothing at the seam. This breadth may also be gored at the top so as to sit quite plain without pleats or gathers in front. The half breadth is placed at the right side. N.B. For small sizes, or where economy is an object, 2 breadths may be used instead of 2½.

The length is ruled according to Fashion or taste; we may however as a general rule say; it should be about 15 inches in front and 24 at back, longer than the skirt of a dress. It is plaited on a waistband, which fastens by hooks and eyes.

LADIES' RIDING TROWSERS.

Fig. 10 shows the manner of cutting Ladies'

(Plate 22.)

Riding Trowsers, and is we believe the first pattern or diagram of the kind ever published.

The measures to take, are 3 in number:—

Waist: taken very tight. *Hips*; measured tight round the outside of the dress. *Side Length;* measured from the waist to the bottom of skirt.

For the DRAFT TO MEASURE. Draw first the construction or Plumb line, and mark on it from 0 to A the Side Length to measure.

From A to B, mark half the Hip measure for the height of fork line. From B to C, half the Hips. From B to D, one quarter of the hips.

Mark in from A, ½ inch for the slope of seat, draw a straight line from D to F, and from the curves of this seam and of the fork, as shown on the diagram. A to F being 7 inches.

A to E; 1½ inch more than half the waist. F to G; 1½ inch more than half the waist.

This 1½ inch extra, is allowed on each side for the buttonholes, by which the Trowsers are to be attached to buttons sewn on the corset; the side seams are left open from C to G, the seat and fork seams being sewn up.

BOYS' COSTUMES.

(Plates 23 and 24.)

The draft for Boys' Costumes, may be rendered simpler than for coats. Boys as a rule, are Long-bodied and rather stout at waist;—comparatively stouter waisted, in proportion as the Breast measures are less: the stooping and extra erect structures are hardly ever met with, and there is but little change in shoulders.

The only measures therefore that need in most cases be taken, are—*Breast*, not taken too tight; *Waist*; *and Length of back to* natural *Waist*. *Front Length* for a Waistcoat. *Leg seam and Hips* for Trowsers.

MANNER OF DRAFTING.

Select a Graduated Measure corresponding to the Breast measure of the boy; taking care never to select one smaller than his measure; in fact it is a good plan to select a measure nearly half an inch larger, because boys often grow so fast, that a garment cut exact to their size would very soon become too small. Boys

(Plates 23 and 24.)

also require plenty of ease for movement, on account of their active habits.

For a JACKET; select any of the patterns on these plates, according to the style required, and draft it as it is, by the Graduated measures. Then apply the *Waist* measure, and enlarge it or reduce it if required, by adding or taking off equal quantities, at the bottom of side and of front edge. Then apply the *Length of back to* natural waist, and if the pattern is not correct, lengthen it or shorten it as required.

For a WAISTCOAT:—After having drafted the pattern, apply the measure of *Front Length*, and lengthen or shorten the waist if required. Correct the waist by the *Waist* measure.

For TROWSERS:—Rule the *Leg Seam* to measure, and mark all the other points by a graduated measure of the size of Hips. Give half the *Waist* measure to the front, and half to the back.

For KNICKERBOCKERS:—Draft the pattern by a Graduated measure corresponding to the size of *Hips*; they will always be right without any correction, except that of the *Waist* measure.

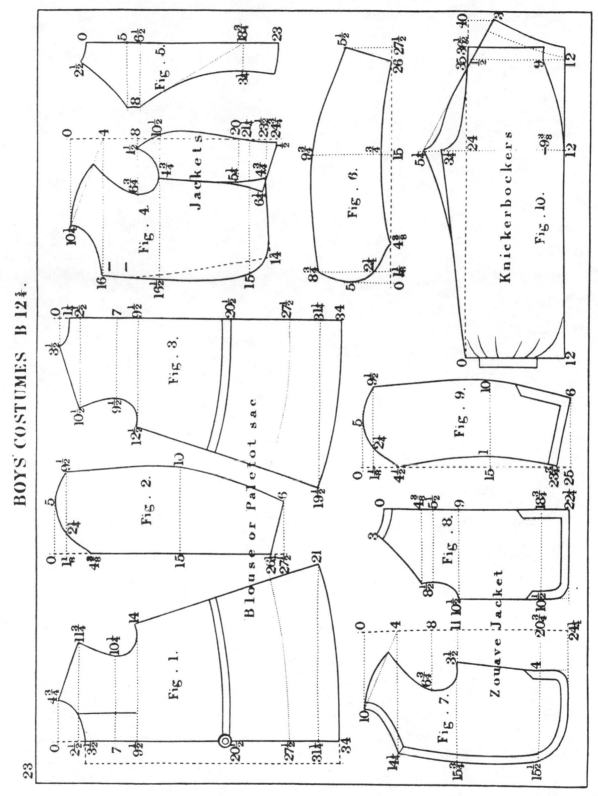

BOYS' COSTUMES B 12¼.

Fig. 5.

Fig. 4.

Jackets

Fig. 6.

Knickerbockers

Fig. 10.

Fig. 3.

Fig. 2.

Blouse or Paletot sac

Fig. 9.

Fig. 8.

Zouave Jacket

Fig. 1.

Fig. 7.

23

VARIOUS STYLES.

(*Plate 23*).

It would of course be impossible in this condensed Work, to give every kind of garments worn by Boys, which are continually varying according to Fashion. We have however classified them, and have given those principal or standard styles, that will always be of service.

These patterns on *plate 23*, are those most suited for the smaller sizes. Those on *plate 24*, are for the larger sizes, say from 14¼ to 15 or 15¾ breast. Sizes above this, we class as Youth's, and they are drafted as for Coats.

PLATE 23. BREAST 12¾.

Figs, 1, 2, and 3, are a BLOUSE: this style is often required, and it is generally made without seam in the front: an opening being made at the side, to pass the head through. It is generally confined at the waist by a belt, as shown on the diagrams, at 20¼. The skirt may vary in length according to Fashion, but is at present generally preferred at 27¼ as shown by the dotted line. The Blouse may be worn either with knickerbockers or short trowsers.

(*Plate 23*.)

A BOY'S PALETOT SAC, may be cut from this pattern, by cutting the skirt longer like the plain lines, adding a lapel of any width, as shown by the long dotted lines, and putting a collar, like fig. 4, in *plate 24.*

Figs. 4, 5, and 6 show two styles of JACKET, made to fasten at the throat only, by two buttons. The Jacket shown by the dotted line at the front edge, is more cut away and has the corner left square. Underneath, a waistcoat without collar may be worn, see figs. 5 and 6, *plate 24.* These jackets may be worn either with knickerbockers, or trowsers.

Figs. 7, 8, and 9 are the ZOUAVE JACKET, usually worn with knickerbockers. It fastens at the throat by a hook and eye, and two buttons and loops on each side. It falls square, and may be trimmed with silk braid laid on flat, as shown on the diagram.

Fig. 10 are the KNICKERBOCKERS; the waistband is cut with them; they are to be gathered into a band which is fastened just below the knee.

N.B. The smallest size in our collection of

(Plate 23.)

Graduated measures, is 12¾, and less sizes than this will be but rarely required. If smaller sizes are wanted, a graduated measure of double the required size must be used, and we must in drafting, only mark half the numbers shown on the diagrams. For instance: if it is wished to draft fig. 1, for a 10½ Breast; take the measure marked B 21, (or double 10½) and mark on the construction line, 0, 1¼, 1¾, 3½, 4¾, &c., &c., which are the halves of 2½, 3½, 7, 9½, &c.; and so on for the rest of the pattern.

PLATE 24. BREAST 14¼.

Figs. 1, 2, 3 and 4, taking the *plain lines* on figs. 1 and 2 for the waist seam, are the ROUND JACKET, a style very generally worn by boys, and often called a Full Dress Jacket. There is a collar and short turnover like a coat, but it may be made of the shawl form like a waistcoat if preferred. The pocket is usually placed out side on the left Breast. The back forms a point at waist. A shawl collar waistcoat and trowsers are generally worn with this jacket.

Figs. 1, 2, 3, and 4, taking the dotted lines

(Plate 24).

at bottom of figs. 1 and 2, are a SKIRTED JACKET; it is very similar to the round jacket in form, but much longer waisted, and is generally worn with trowsers and waistcoat of the straight form.

Figs. 5 and 6 are a WAISTCOAT, which has a collar of the shawl form, or may be made of the straight form without collar, or indeed may take any of the forms shown on *plates* 15 and 16.

Figs. 7 and 8, with the collar, fig. 4, and the sleeve in *plate* 23, fig. 2, are a PALETOT JACKET, falling nearly square. Boys' jackets of this style, are usually cut with the skirts rather short, as shown by the dotted lines. In the forepart, the fish under the arm may be omitted if the garment is required looser fitting. The Back may be made with or without seam in the middle.

This same pattern will also serve for a Boy's OVERCOAT, by making the skirts the full length.

Fig. 9 is the TROWSERS, which have the waist-band cut with them, and which for Boys are usually made rather high at the waist. It will be observed that the right and left points of fork, are at 3⅛ for both sides.

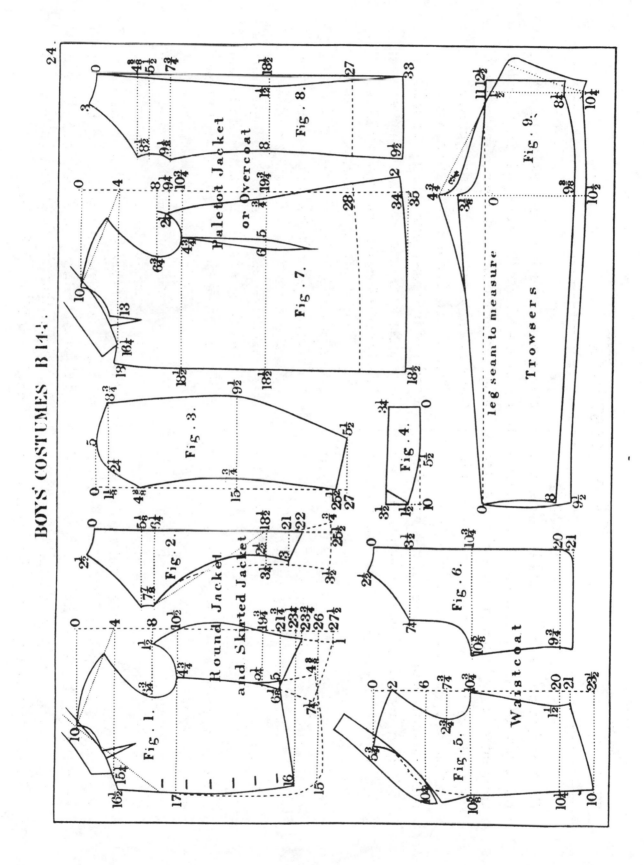

BOYS' COSTUMES B 14.

HANDBOOK OF PRACTICAL CUTTING.

PART THE THIRD.

OVERCOATS.

(Plate 25.)

THE draft of Overcoats is a branch of the Art of Cutting, which has hitherto received but little attention from those who have written on the subject. Some, have simply directed the student to draft the garment for a size larger than the real breast measure of the client, apparently not being aware that an Overcoat, as compared with a close-fitting coat, requires, not a general increase of size, but extra allowances in certain parts only. Others have merely given the patterns of Overcoats for what they term a proportionate man, and have provided no means of varying the form of the pattern, to suit the many different builds,

(Plate 25.)

which are met with alike for Overcoats of all styles, the same as for coats.

This branch of the Art of Cutting, we have made the subject of special and careful study, and we think it of such great importance, that we have devoted an entire part of this work to its explanation.

An Overcoat is a garment which is intended to be worn over another coat, and which must therefore, have certain extra quantities of stuff allowed in certain parts, to permit of its being so worn. There are many styles of Overcoat, varying from those which fit nearly as tight as a Frock coat, to those which have almost as great a degree of fulness as a Cloak; and these various styles of Overcoats are known by many names:—names which vary every season, and

L

(*Plate 25.*)

which consequently would be quite out of place, in a standard work like the present. We have, therefore, divided all the known styles of Overcoats, into three general types, which will and have described them by names, which will we think, be easily recognized and understood by the whole of our readers.

First. The TOP COAT, cut like a Frock Coat, with a seam across at the waist, and generally made as close-fitting as is consistent with comfort to the wearer. This style is by some persons, called a Frock-overcoat or a Great Coat.

Second. The PALETOT, by which name we understand all garments that are made WITH-OUT *a seam across* at the waist, and which in consequence have the skirt and side body cut in one piece with the forepart. We use the term PALETOT, to all garments cut in this manner, whether they are as tight-fitting as a Top Coat, are of only medium width, or are cut so as to fall perfectly square without defining the waist at all. This style by some tailors is

(*Plate 25.*)

generally called a Chesterfield or a close-fitting Wrapper.

Third. LOOSE OVERCOATS. In this class we include all those styles of Overcoat which are cut without seam at waist, but which, instead of falling square, have an extra degree of fulness, either behind, in front, or at the sides, and which require extra allowances beyond those necessary for a Paletot. An Overcoat of this style, is called by many persons, a Sac, a *Paletot-sac*, a Driving Coat, or a loose Wrapper.

After having explained the manner of drafting all these garments, we shall describe the cut of Capes and Cloaks, of all the kinds now in use, and give easy and exact instructions for drafting them to measure for all styles, and will terminate this part of our work, by an easy system for drafting all the principal kinds of Paletots and Sleeved Mantles for Ladies, which have lately become so important a branch of some trades.

MEASUREMENT.

(Plate 25.)

The measures which are to be taken for an ordinary coat. For men of very disproportionate structure, they are divided into two principal series and a supplementary one, all of which will be found fully described in Part 1, *plate 4*, pages 8 to 12. In almost every case, however, it will be quite sufficient to take SEVEN MEASURES ONLY, viz. :—

No. 1.—BREAST taken *on the Waistcoat* in the usual way.

No. 2.—WAIST also taken on the Waistcoat.

No. 3.—CURVE ⎫
No. 4.—BUST ⎬ as described in Part 1.
No. 5.—SIDE ⎭

The LENGTH OF SLEEVE, measured from the middle of back to the wrist.

The FULL LENGTH, to the bottom of skirt.

Nos. 1 to 5 constitute the *first series* of Measures (see page 9), and they should NEVER BE OMITTED to be taken; as it is by them that

(Plate 25.)

all the principal points of the pattern are drafted. The length to the wrist also, should always be taken, because the arm varies considerably in different men. It is also a good plan to measure the length to the bottom, so as to make sure that the Overcoat may have sufficient length to cover the skirt of the undercoat.

The length of back to the hip buttons, and the widths of sleeve at elbow and wrist, may also be taken if preferred; but these points are dependent solely on Fashion, and may as a rule, be left to the taste or judgment of the Cutter, who should be guided by the diagrams published monthly in our *Magazine of Fashion.*

As regards the Third or *supplementary* series of measures; it need only be taken in those rare cases, in which a client is found to differ very greatly from the proportionate structure : it will, however, in many instances, be found a good plan to take the measure called *Slope of Shoulder,* or else to notice if the client has his shoulders higher or lower than the proportionate build.

(Plate 25.)

The measures we have named above, are to be taken for all styles of Top Coats, and Paletots and also Loose Overcoats, excepting the extremely loose sleeved Cloaks, in which it will suffice to take the Breast and Waist measures, and the full length, and to note whether the man is Stooping or Extra-erect, and if his shoulders are High or Low.

Before entering into the details of the subject, we will remark that in this Handbook, we have given two ways of drafting Top Coats and Paletots.

The *first* consists in drawing the close-fitting pattern of the client, as explained in Part 1, and then adding to this pattern when drafted, certain extra quantities, which will allow of its being worn over an undercoat. This is of course a good and quick way, if you have already drafted your client's pattern for an undercoat. Again, if the structure is extremely disproportionate, the Overcoat should be drafted in this manner.

(Plate 25.)

The *second* plan is that which will be found the most convenient, and the most certain for all ordinary structures, and is that which will we think be most generally preferred. The back and forepart are drafted side by side in two squares, as for coats, an additional width being given to each of the squares; and other allowances or modifications being made where required, as we will now proceed to explain for each particular style.

TOP COATS.

The Top Coat with seam at waist, is the simplest to understand of all the styles of Overcoat. It is nothing more than a Frock Coat, to which certain quantities are added to make it fit over another coat.

These extra allowances are explained by figs. 1 and 2; the fine dotted line showing the close-fitting pattern or wrapper of the body, and the plain line giving the form of the Top Coat, after the requisite additions have been made.

(*Plate 25.*)

The *back* must have about $\frac{3}{8}$ of an inch *added all along the middle*, from top to bottom, without changing the lengths or the relative position of any of the widths. The *forepart* must have $\frac{1}{2}$ *an inch extra width allowed at the front edge*, from top to bottom. Besides this the *bottom of scye* must be about $\frac{3}{8}$ *of an inch more hollowed out*, so as to make the armhole larger, and so give more length to the shoulder-strap.

This extra hollowing out given to the bottom of scye, merits particular attention. It has the effect of lengthening the shoulder-piece a quantity, which although small, is nevertheless sufficient, because the back neck of a Top Coat is $2\frac{3}{4}$ wide (instead of $2\frac{5}{8}$), and the enlargement of this part contributes to the lengthening of the shoulder-piece: at the same time, deepening the scye causes the side point to become relatively higher, thus counterbalancing the extra length given to the shoulder-piece, and preventing the balance of the pattern from being in any way deranged.

(*Plate 25.*)

The Waist of course will require lengthening in the same way as for a Frock Coat, see Part 1, *plate* 8, page 24. It will now be at once seen that if we have already the close-fitting pattern of a client, we can at once convert it into a Top Coat by a few strokes of the chalk; making the front edge and the back, respectively $\frac{1}{2}$ an inch and $\frac{3}{8}$ wider, deepening the scye $\frac{3}{8}$ of an inch, and lengthening the waist as required.

The Proportionate Pattern.

The numbers of construction on figs. 1 and 2 give the proportionate pattern of a Top Coat, of the most elegant style. This pattern will be found very useful in practice, as if any of the required measures have not been taken, the figures of the proportionate pattern are those which have the most chance of being correct. Besides this, many houses always keep a few Top Coats ready made, and these should of course be cut from the proportionate model.

(*Plate* 25.)

We will now examine the details of this pattern.

In the *Back*, fig. 2; The lengths are precisely the same as for an ordinary coat (see fig. 1, *plate* 3). We have $3\frac{7}{8}$ and 5, for the top and bottom of back scye, and $17\frac{1}{4}$ for the waist. The *Balance*, or distance of the top of back from the corner of square, is also without change, because the difference between the lengths of natural waist in back and forepart ($17\frac{1}{4}$ and $19\frac{3}{4}$) is $2\frac{1}{2}$. The widths however are all increased $\frac{3}{8}$ of an inch; the back neck being at $2\frac{3}{4}$ instead of $2\frac{3}{8}$, the back stretch being $8\frac{1}{4}$ wide instead of $7\frac{7}{8}$, and the width at waist being $2\frac{3}{4}$ instead of $2\frac{3}{8}$.

In the *Forepart*, fig. 1. The Slope and the height of Side-point are without change; the Bottom of scye is at $10\frac{3}{8}$ instead of 10, thus showing that the scye is deepened $\frac{3}{8}$ of an inch; the Hollow of the hips and Bottom of side, $18\frac{1}{2}$ and $19\frac{3}{4}$, showing that the position of these points remains unaltered. For the widths:—the shoulder point remains without

(*Plate* 25.)

change at $9\frac{1}{2}$: the Side point, the Diameter of arm, the hollowest part of Scye, and the Centre point, are exactly the same as for a Dress or Frock Coat. The figures at the front edge, however, are $14\frac{3}{4}$, $16\frac{1}{4}$, 15, instead of $14\frac{1}{4}$, $15\frac{3}{4}$, $14\frac{1}{4}$, as in a close-fitting garment, thus showing that $\frac{1}{2}$ an inch is added at the front edge, from the neck to below the breast line, and $\frac{3}{4}$ at the bottom; it is $\frac{3}{4}$ at the bottom, on account of the extra lengthening given to the Waist.

The curves in Overcoats are always drawn as explained in Part 1, *plate* 3.

DRAFT TO MEASURE.

The draft to measure is based precisely on the same principles as that of coats. The back and forepart are placed side by side in two squares. These squares are, however, for Top Coats, each made wider than for coats, so that the pattern when drafted may have all the necessary extra width, without any trouble or calculation. The compartment that contains the forepart must be made $\frac{1}{4}$ a graduated inch

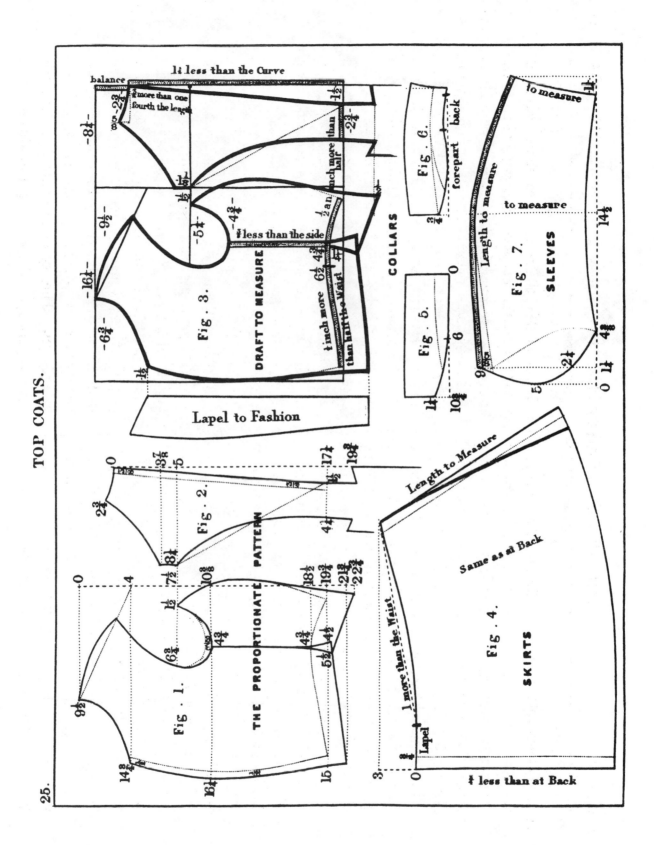

TOP COATS.

25.

Fig. 3.

DRAFT TO MEASURE

1¼ less than the Curve

balance

⅞ more than one fourth the length

Lapel to Fashion

COLLARS

Fig. 6.

forepart   back

Fig. 5.

Fig. 7.

SLEEVES

to measure

Length to measure

to measure

Fig. 1.

THE PROPORTIONATE PATTERN

Fig. 2.

Length to Measure

Fig. 4.

SKIRTS

Same as at Back

1 more than the Waist

Lapel

¼ less than at Back

(Plate 25.)

wider ($16\frac{1}{4}$ instead of $15\frac{3}{4}$), and the compartment for the back, $\frac{3}{8}$ wider, ($8\frac{1}{4}$ instead of $7\frac{7}{8}$). This being done, the Draft is formed exactly in the same way as for a Frock Coat.

Fig. 3. First with a graduated measure corresponding to the breast measure of the client, form two squares or compartments, one having a width of $8\frac{1}{4}$, the other $16\frac{1}{4}$. Then take the common inch measure, and starting from the corner of the smallest compartment, measure downwards, the *Balance* or difference between the *Bust* and *Curve* measures, to find the top of back. Starting from this point, mark $1\frac{1}{2}$ graduated inches less than the *Curve* measure, for the length of back to natural waist: draw a line square across at the bottom. Then measure downwards from the top of back, $\frac{3}{4}$ more than a fourth part of the length, for the bottom of back stretch, and draw a line square across into the larger compartment: this will give the height of Side point. Then mark from the bottom $1\frac{1}{4}$ graduated inches up to find the hollow of the hips, and starting

(Plate 25.)

from the Centre point, rule the length of Side at $\frac{3}{8}$ less than the measure.

All the fixed points of the pattern are ruled by the figures shown on the diagram.

For the *Waist*; take the middle at $6\frac{1}{2}$, and starting from this point give $\frac{1}{2}$ an inch more than half the measure to the forepart, and $\frac{1}{2}$ an inch more than half to the side body and back. The Waist is lengthened in the usual way, first lengthening the back to Fashion or taste, and drawing a line square across to meet the bottom of side, which point should come a little below this line, to allow for the seam at back plait: $\frac{1}{2}$ an inch is a very good degree of extra lengthening for the side body, as shown on the diagram. The lengthening of forepart, is usually from $\frac{1}{4}$ to $\frac{1}{2}$ an inch less than that of the back.

LAPELS.

The Lapel of a Top Coat is drafted exactly the same as that of a Frock Coat, except that it has a width of from 3 to 4 inches at the top, and from $2\frac{1}{2}$ to $3\frac{1}{2}$ at the bottom. These widths

(Plate 25.)

are continually varying according to Fashion. Single-breasted Top Coats with the skirts cut separate, are now very rarely made, but if required the front edge should be cut as shown by fig. 6, *plate* 9.

SKIRTS, FIG. 4.

These are drawn as for a Frock Coat, but making it a little wider at the top. Draw the Construction line and mark from 0 upwards, the degree of slope required according to Fashion or taste (see fig. 4, *plate* 10). Then mark square across from 0; $\frac{3}{4}$ for the plait, and then the width of the lapel, and rule the length of the top of skirt at 1 more than the size of the waist. The slope of back plait is ruled to agree with the side body (fig. 1, *plate* 26), but as Overcoats are generally rather long, a little less fulness may be given at the bottom, gradating to nothing at about 4 inches from the waist, as shown by the strong black line. The lengths and bottom are drawn as shown on the diagram. The draft of back skirts is explained in Part 1.

COLLARS.

(Plate 25.)

Fig. 5 shows the ordinary form of collar, having a length of about $10\frac{3}{4}$, or $\frac{3}{4}$ more than for an ordinary coat. The front part of neck is sloped $1\frac{1}{4}$, and the stand, fall, and shape of front end, are drawn to Fashion or taste.

Fig. 6 shows another form of collar, well suited either for very long turnovers, or for being worn turned down all round. The front corner is sloped $\frac{3}{4}$ upwards, and the back is a little hollowed out, say $\frac{1}{4}$ or $\frac{3}{8}$. This diagram shows the best way of ruling the length of a collar: starting from the front corner, mark first the length of the neck seam of forepart, then the length of neck seam of the back, and cut the collar about $\frac{1}{2}$ an inch longer than this: this extra half inch is for the seams and working up, &c.; it would be a great fault to cut a collar too short, but a little extra length is easily remedied.

Collars for Paletots, and all styles of Over-coats, may be drafted in this way.

SLEEVES, FIG. 7.

(*Plate 25.*)

Draw first the Construction line, and on it mark 1¼, 4⅜, and 14½: draw lines square across. Then mark on the first line 5, and on the second 2¼ and 9, graduated inches: Point 9 is the top of hind arm, and from this point rule the Length of Sleeve to measure, of course deducting the width of back stretch. The widths at elbow and wrist are ruled to measure or to Fashion, the slope at bottom of wrist being about 1¼.

Of course the sleeves of all Overcoats are subject to all the changes of Fashion, shown on fig. 4, *plate* 9, Part 1.

SKIRT CUT
IN ONE PIECE WITH THE FOREPART.

(*Plate 26.*)

There is one style of Overcoat, that seems to partake of the nature both of the Top Coat and Paletot: it has the skirt cut in one piece

(*Plate 26.*)

with the forepart and lapel, while the side body is joined in separate, in the same way as the Morning Coat on *plate* 11 of Part 1. This style of coat is usually made single-breasted, closing with fly front, and rather looser-fitting at waist than a Top Coat: it is this style which was generally known some years ago, as the Nicoll Paletot. It must, however, be classed among the Top Coats, because it is drafted in precisely the same manner, and the special changes which have to be made for Paletots, do not in the least apply to this style of garment.

The draft to measure is the same as fig. 3, *plate* 25, except that the skirt is drawn at the bottom of the forepart, and that a little extra length must be given all along the bottom of side body, to allow for the slight increase of length given to the forepart by the seam at the top of skirt.

The draft of the sleeve and collar, is of course the same as that shown on *plate* 25, which we have just described.

M

PALETOTS.

(*Plate* 26.)

The Paletot is a garment which was almost unknown in this country, at the time we first introduced our system to the English public. Since that time it has been steadily increasing in public favor, and is every season becoming more and more widely adopted.

The Paletot may be termed one of the most elegant styles of Overcoat, and the one which is the best calculated to suit all figures, all classes, and all ages. It may be cut of every degree of fulness: there is the close-fitting style, so well calculated to display the graceful figure of youth and early manhood; there is the medium style, which, while it displays the figure to the best advantage, combines that ease and comfort desired by those who have arrived at maturity; we have the square-cut style, so generally preferred by men who are given to athletic sports, from the great facility which it gives for muscular action; and lastly there are the looser-fitting styles, so admirably

(*Plate* 26.)

adapted for men of middle age, who have arrived at a certain degree of corpulency.

There are other circumstances which have also had some influence, in creating a preference for this style of garment: it is more economical both in wear and in cost. The absence of the seam at waist renders it less liable to show the effects of wear, and the same reason materially reduces the cost of making up, thus rendering it profitable alike to the buyer and to the seller. The one difficulty, which has in some degree retarded the general adoption of the Paletot, is the uncertainty which has hitherto prevailed, as to the principles on which it should be cut. In order, therefore, fully to establish correct ideas and rules, we have devoted nearly half the plates contained in this Part, to the explanation of all the styles of this elegant garment, and of the correct manner of drafting it for all sizes and structures, and for every degree of fulness.

The system here given is based upon the results of careful reasoning and of innumerable

(Plate 26.)

measurements and experiments, and its accuracy and certainty in practice has been thoroughly tested. It possesses this great advantage over all other methods :—that for all structures and for all styles, from the closest fitting to those falling perfectly square, the draft is formed precisely in the same manner.

The measures themselves rule all the principal points of the pattern.

The fixed points are ruled by the graduated measures for all sizes and all structures.

The style, the fulness, and the relative position of seams, while still subject to certain fixed rules, are modified of themselves, according to Fashion or the taste of the cutter, and in no change of Fashion or of style, can have the slightest effect in deranging the balance or the harmony of the garment.

GENERAL PRINCIPLES.

We have first to call the attention of our readers, to a few important modifications, or differences from the ordinary pattern, which

(Plate 26.)

have to be made in drafting a Paletot, and which are shown on figs. 3 and 4 of *plate* 26.

We will first state as briefly as possible, what these alterations are, and will afterwards give a few additional explanations as to the reasons for which they are made.

FIRST, and most important of all :—The *Balance* for all Paletots, is to be ruled at $\frac{3}{4}$ LESS than the difference between the *Bust* and *Curve* measures ; that is to say, the top of back is $\frac{3}{4}$ higher up in the square (see fig. 4). This is to compensate for the fish under the arm.

SECOND. The *Side Point* being as usual placed on the same level as the bottom of back stretch, will of course also be $\frac{3}{4}$ higher up in the square than for a Top Coat; see the plain line of figs. 3 and 4, in which the side points are respectively placed at $7\frac{1}{2}$ and $6\frac{3}{4}$, measured down the construction lines of forepart.

THIRD. The *Taking in of Side Point* is always marked at $1\frac{3}{4}$ for all Paletots (see fig. 4).

FOURTH. The *Side* measure (see fig. 4) is always marked upwards from the waist line,

(Plate 26.)

and not as for coats, from the real place of the centre point, which would be half an inch above this line.

FIFTH. The *Waist* measure is ruled by giving 1 more than the measure at front, and 2½ more at the back. Take the middle of waist at 6½, as a starting point (see fig. 4), and mark one more than half the waist, to rule the place of front edge. Give the other half of the waist measure, for the side body, at point A, and then the 2½ extra for the width of back at waist (point A). Out of this 2½ extra, 1½ is to compensate for the loss produced by the fish taken out under the arm, and 1 is for the inch of extra width required in a Paletot, to correspond with that given to the forepart. Those two last named points, A, A, in fig. 4, are always marked for all Paletots, and serve as points of departure, one to control the extra width given to the back according to style or Fashion, and the other to determine the degree of additional fulness given to the garment.

We will now a little more fully explain the

(Plate 26.)

various reasons which render these changes necessary.

Fig. 3. We have before shown that for long waists, the forepart and side body must be sprung out at the bottom of the seam under the arm, to give room for the prominence of the hips. In a Paletot, however, the only way of providing for this prominence, is to take out a long fish under the arm, 1½ wide at waist, and to compensate for this fish, the side body must be displaced, as shown by the strong black line, by which it will be seen that the side point is raised up ¾ of an inch, and is advanced to 2 from the construction line.

Fig. 4. As the bottom of back scye should always be on the same level as the side point, the back must be altogether raised up ¾ higher in the square, and this will of course make the *Balance* ¾ less than the difference between the *Bust and Curve*,—1¾, in fig. 4, instead of 2½, as in fig. 3, and so on for all sizes and structures. The back being drafted as usual without change of form, the bottom of back scye,

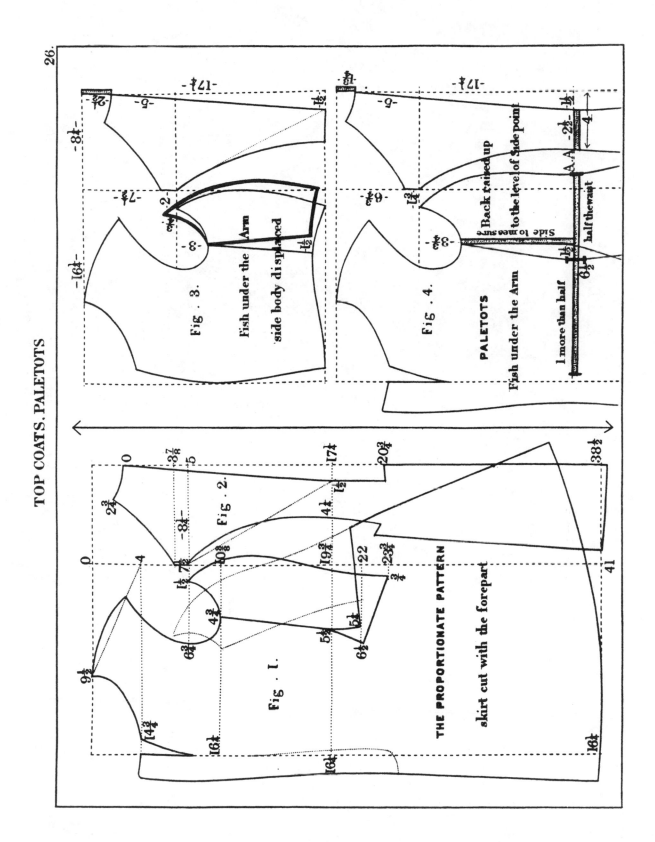

Fig . 1.

THE PROPORTIONATE PATTERN

skirt cut with the forepart

Fig . 2.

Fig . 3.

Fish under the Arm

side body displaced

Fig . 4.

PALETOTS

Fish under the Arm

Back raised up to the leve of Side point

Side to measure

1 more than half

half the waist

(*Plate* 26.)

and consequently the side point, will thus of themselves become ¾ higher, without making the special change shown on fig. 3.

The taking in of side point is placed at 1¾, instead of at 2 as in fig. 3, because a Paletot requires a little extra width at this part.

The depth of scye below the side point, is at 3¾ for the proportionate man: it will of course be more than this for Stooping men, and less for Extra-erect ones.

The points of the side body and back in fig. 4, called A, A, are very important, and are to be always marked in drafting a Paletot, no matter what the required fulness or width of back may be.

In the back, point A is always marked at a distance of 4 graduated inches from the outside line of square; 1½ of this is for the slope of the seam in the middle, and 2½ is for the width of back at waist, and this is the *least width* that can be given to the back of a Paletot. The manner of giving any extra width will be explained hereafter.

(*Plate* 26.)

Point A of the Side Body, is always marked at a distance of half the waist measure, from the middle of waist at 6½. It indicates the greatest degree in which the seam must be sprung out beyond the construction line, for a close-fitting Paletot.

When we have these two points fixed, we can alter the place of side seam in any way we please (as explained in Part 1, *plate* 8, fig. 2). We can make the back wider, and the side body narrower. We can allow on the side body, any extra degree of fulness that may be required, and are able to calculate exactly how much fulness is allowed; and no matter in what style the Paletot may be cut, the side seams of forepart and back will always be in harmony and accordance with each other.

This pattern (fig. 4) shows the simplest form that can be given to a Close-fitting Paletot. It is a style, however, which at the present time is hardly ever required, and we think the back should always be cut wider for this kind of garment.

(Plate 26.)

Having thus explained the general principles on which all Paletots should be cut, we will now proceed to describe the details of the system.

THE PROPORTIONATE PATTERN.

(Plate 27.)

Figs. 1 and 2 give the pattern of a Paletot, for the Proportionate Structure. The style is one which is very often required, and has what we call a medium degree of extra width, that is to say, it is cut so as slightly to define the waist, without fitting quite tight to the figure. The close-fitting coat pattern is shown by the fine dotted line. It will be seen that the back scye has an extra depth of about 2 inches (from 5 to 7), and the top of side point, while drawn to correspond with the lowered place of the back stretch, is nevertheless, placed about ⅛ an inch above it, so as to give extra fulness at this part. The fish under the arm has a width of 1½ at the waist, it might have a less width

than this, if preferred, say 1¼ or 1 inch only; or it might be entirely omitted if a looser style of Paletot was required. Fig. 5 gives the proportionate pattern of a Sleeve suited for this pattern, and indeed for all the Paletots and Paletot Jackets contained in *plates* 26 to 29.

HOW TO DRAFT FROM A CLOSE-FITTING PATTERN. FIGS. 1 & 2.

A Paletot may be cut from the close-fitting pattern of a coat, and though this manner of drafting is rather more difficult than that we are about to explain presently, it may sometimes be advisable to draft the Paletot in this manner; for instance, if the client has an extremely disproportionate structure, or if we have his close-fitting pattern all ready cut. It is explained by figs. 1 and 2;—the back, side body, and forepart shown by the fine dotted line, are the close-fitting wrapper of the body, as explained in Part 1, and the small figures near it, show the differences to make in order to convert it into a Paletot.

(Plate 27.)

For the Back. First allow ⅜ extra, all down the middle; then lower the back stretch any quantity, say 2 inches, and widen it at waist according to Fashion, giving for instance, about 3 inches extra as in this diagram. The curves of side seam and the back skirt, may now be drawn according to Fashion.

For the Forepart. Give an extra width to the front edge of ½ an inch at the top, ½ at the chest, and 1 or 1½ at the waist, and draw the lapel according to Fashion. Next make the scye ½ an inch deeper, take out a fish of 1½ under the arm, and displace the side body as shown on fig. 3, *plate* 26. We must now take off certain quantities from the side body, to compensate for the extra width given to the back: at the top take off 1½, that is to say, ½ less than the quantity that has been added to the back at this part, which was 2 inches. At the waist take off about 1 only, or 2 less than has been added to the back, thus allowing an extra fulness of 2 inches at this part. If a close-fitting Paletot is required, take off nearly

(Plate 27.)

as much as has been added to the back, and for a square-cut style do not take off any at all. It would, however, always be better to rule the width of the waist with more exactness, as explained for fig. 4, *plate* 28, even where the rest of the pattern has been drafted as we have just described. The side seam and the skirt, are of course drawn to Fashion or to taste.

ACCESSORY PIECES.

Before describing the regular Draft to Measure, we will give a few general remarks on SLEEVES and COLLARS, which must be understood to apply to all styles of Paletots and Paletot Jackets, and which may serve to clear up the great uncertainty, so prevalent with some persons, as to the principles on which these pieces should be cut.

COLLARS.

The collars for Paletots, and indeed for Top Coats, are to be cut exactly in the same way as for ordinary coats, except that they are to be about ¾ of an inch longer.

(Plate 27.)

Fig. 3 gives a very simple and easy draft for a *Collar of the Ordinary Form.* Take the forepart, lay it on a sheet of paper, and draw first the Crease Line, from the neck point to the shoulder point, shown by the fine dotted line. Above this, mark the depth required for the fall of collar to Fashion, and shape the end according to taste; then mark the height of stand, and draw the neck seam of collar; the front part follows the neck seam of forepart, for about 4 inches. The length of collar may on an average, be ruled at 3 graduated inches beyond the forepart, as shown on the diagram, or the length may be ruled as shown on fig. 6, *plate 25*, which is the plan we ourselves always use for the collars of all garments.

Fig. 4 shows the manner of obtaining a *Collar of the Shawl form,* a style which is often required for Paletot Jackets, and even for Top Coats and Paletots. Take the forepart, and draw first the straight crease line as explained for fig. 3. Then mark on the front edge, the place at which the bottom of the crease is to

(Plate 27.)

be, and draw the crease line of the shawl to meet the straight line at the shoulder point.

Next draw the neck seam of forepart, lowering the neck point so that it is about 4 inches above the bottom of crease line, and take out a large fish, in the same way as for a waistcoat. The back part of collar is drawn as explained for fig. 3, marking the stand and fall to Fashion, and giving 3 beyond the forepart for the length. The outside of collar is shaped according to Fashion, or the width which it is desired to give to the shawl; the neck seam of collar is first drawn straight from the back; then follows the neck seam of forepart as far as the fish, and from this point it curves a little up, so as to have a closer fit when made up, and to compensate the extra curve given to the neck seam of forepart by the fish.

SLEEVES.

Fig. 5 gives the proportionate pattern of a sleeve, and shows the proportions of width at elbow and wrist, which are suitable for a Top Coat or a Paletot.

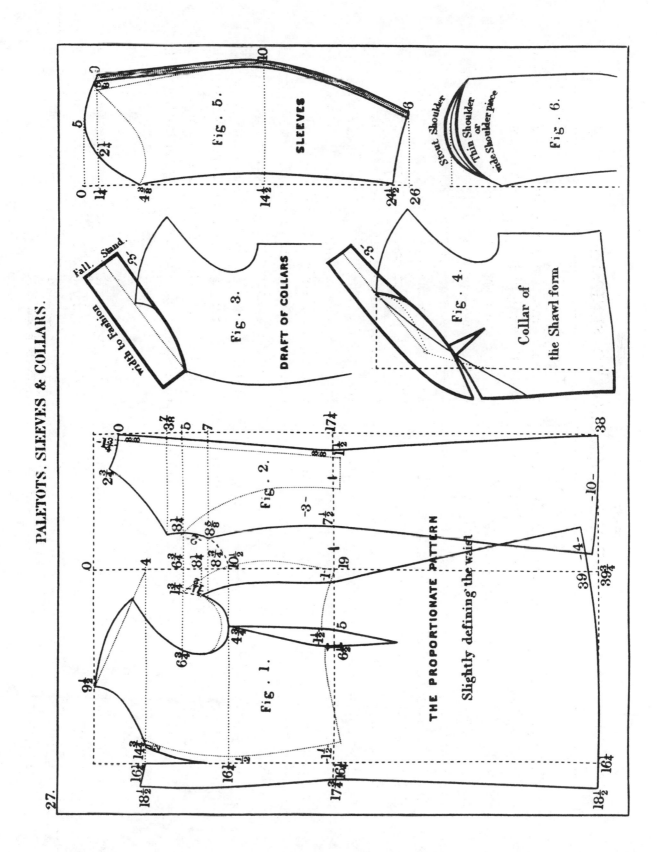

PALETOTS. SLEEVES & COLLARS.

Fig. 5.

SLEEVES

Fig. 6.

Stout Shoulder
Thin Shoulder
or
wide Shoulder piece

Fall. Stand.

width to fashion

Fig. 3.

DRAFT OF COLLARS

Fig. 4.

Collar of
the Shawl form

Fig. 2.

Fig. 1.

THE PROPORTIONATE PATTERN

Slightly defining the waist

27.

(Plate 27.)

The draft of the Sleeve to measure, is very simple. Draw first by the graduated measures, the sleeve head as shown on fig. 5. Then rule the length to wrist according to measure, and mark the widths at elbow and wrist according to Fashion, sloping the wrist from $1\frac{1}{4}$ to $1\frac{1}{2}$ graduated inches.

We draw all Overcoat sleeve heads of the same width, 9 graduated inches, and provide for the greater or less degree of fulness, given to the armholes in different styles, by making the under side a little wider for the looser styles, than is shown on fig. 5; so that for some Paletots, the upper part of the under side of Sleeve may even have the same width as the top side.

Fig. 6 shows that sometimes it may be necessary to give more or less round to the sleeve head. We may give more round for very large muscular shoulders, or if the Fashion requires fulness at this part. We must give less round for very thin shoulders, or if the shoulder-piece of the pattern is very wide, as in a Paletot-sac or Sleeved Cloak.

DRAFT TO MEASURE.

(Plate 28.)

In order to render this part of our subject as clear as possible, we have divided the Draft to Measure into two parts; fig. 1 showing the manner of drawing those parts of the pattern which are the same for all styles, and fig. 2 showing the manner of drawing the side seams of back and forepart, and of varying the relative position of these seams, so as to produce every variety of style and fulness.

FIRST OPERATION, FIG. 1.

This part of the draft is done in a similar way to that which we have already described for Top Coats, of course including in the draft those modifications explained for fig. 4 of *plate* 26. There is this additional difference, however, that the compartment for the back has here a width of 11 graduated inches, instead of $8\frac{1}{4}$ as usual. The square is made thus wider for two reasons:—*First*, because we may have to draft Paletots with backs of every possible degree of width, and 11 gradu-

(*Plate* 28.)

ated inches is the greatest width that can be given to the back scye of a Paletot. *Secondly,* in order that the back and forepart may not lay over each other too much at the bottom.

First form two squares: the one 11 graduated inches wide, the other 16¼ graduated inches, allowing beyond it any degree of width for the lapel. Then mark the *Balance,* at ¾ less than the difference between the *Bust* and *Curve*; rule the *Length* of back at 1½ less than the *Curve*; and the *Full Length* to measure or Fashion. Mark for the bottom of back scye, as usual, at ¾ more than a fourth of the length of back. Draw lines square across at the back scye, the waist, and the bottom.

Then starting from the waist line, measure up the length of side to measure, and draw a line square across, which will give the depth of scye for the forepart, and will indicate the greatest depth at which the back scye in an ordinary Paletot can possibly be pitched. All the other points of the patterns for all sizes and structures, are to be ruled by the graduated

(*Plate* 28.)

measures, and the curves are to be drawn as explained in Part 1. If the *Slope* measure has been taken, mark down the construction line, double the Slope for the shoulder-strap.

N. B.—Be careful to mark the WIDTH of BACK STRETCH AT 8¼ ONLY, and not at the full width of square, as for Top Coats.

The curves of back scye and of the top of side body, are always to be drawn in the first instance, as shown on this diagram, no matter what form it is intended to give to the pattern. For the Side Body, draw a line from the side point to the bottom of scye at 4¾, and hollow in ¾ from this line: for the *Back Scye,* draw a line from the top of side measure to the bottom of back scye, as shown on the diagram, and hollow in ¾ from this line.

For the *Waist*: first mark the middle point at 6½, and rule the width of front, by putting along the waist line 1 more than half the measure. Then mark half the waist for the greatest width of side body, as before explained, and starting from the construction line of back,

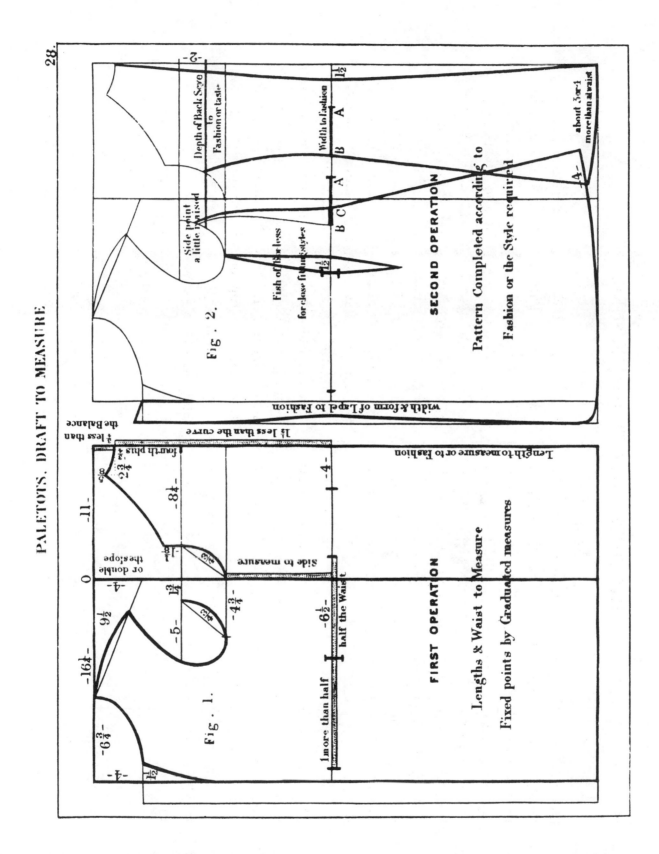

Fig. 2.

SECOND OPERATION

Pattern Completed according to

Fashion or the Style required

Depth of Back Scye
to
Fashion or taste

Width to fashion

A

B C A

B C

Side point
a little Raised

Fish of Fish less
for close fitting styles

$\frac{1}{12}$

$1\frac{1}{2}$

about 3 or 4
more than at waist

$4-$

Width & form of Lapel to Fashion

$2-$

Fig. 1.

FIRST OPERATION

Lengths & Waist to Measure

Fixed points by Graduated measures

Length to measure or to Fashion

$\frac{3}{4}$ less than
the Balance

$1\frac{1}{2}$ less than the curve

fourth plus $\frac{3}{4}$

$8-$

$2\frac{1}{4}$

$-8\frac{1}{4}$

$-11-$

or double
the slope

$-1\frac{1}{8}$

$3\frac{1}{2}$

$-5-$

$-1\frac{3}{4}$

$3\frac{1}{2}$

$-4\frac{3}{4}$

Side to measure

$-4-$

0

$-4-$

$-9\frac{1}{2}$

$-16\frac{1}{4}-$

$-6\frac{3}{4}$

$-4-$

$1\frac{1}{2}$

half the Waist

$-6\frac{1}{2}-$

1 more than half

(Plate 28.)

mark 4 graduated inches for the least width that the back can have.

SECOND OPERATION, FIG. 2.

We have now to complete the pattern by drawing the *Side seams*, the *Bottom*, and the *Lapel*, and this is done in a few minutes, as shown by fig. 2.

THE BACK.

First mark in 1½ for the slope at waist, unless a looser-fitting style is required, in which case less slope may be given, or even none at all, so as to leave extra width at this part. Then mark on the construction line of back, the extra depth it is intended the back scye should have, say 1, 2, 2½, or 3 graduated inches. Draw a line square at this point, crossing the curves of back scye and top of side body, and thus giving the important points of the bottom of Back Scye, and the top of Side, for a Paletot. Next mark the whole width required for the back at waist, or the extra width from point A to B, and rule the width of bottom, say at 3 or 4

(Plate 28.)

more than the width at waist. Draw the curve of side seam, through the points marked; it is generally in a straight line from the waist to the bottom. The curve at the bottom is raised up a little from the square line.

THE FOREPART.

First take out a fish under the arm of 1½ or less, according as a close-fitting or medium style is wanted. For a square-cut style, omit the fish.

Next mark the side point, a trifle higher up than the square line which rules the depth of back scye. It is raised up higher, so as to give a little more ease to the scye, for the movements of the arm. For a tight-fitting style, it is usual to raise it up ¼ inch only, or perhaps less, while for the medium and square-cut styles, it may be raised ½ or even ¾ of an inch.

To fix the place of side seam at the waist ; take the back, and measure first the distance between point A and the side seam at point B. Then starting from point A, of the forepart, measure to point B, the same distance as the distance between A, B, of the back ; this will give

(*Plate* 28)

the exact place at which the side seam should be drawn, for a tight-fitting Paletot. If any extra fulness is required at the waist, say 1, 2, or 3 inches, or about 1½ as in this diagram, this extra fulness is added to the side body, from B to C, and gives the exact place at which the side seam is to be drawn.

For the bottom; mark the width according to Fashion, and the style or fulness required, and raise up the bottom corner a little above the back, to compensate for the extra height given to the side point. Draw the curves of side seam and the bottom, by the hand as usual.

The Lapel is marked according to Fashion: it is generally curved in at the waist for the close-fitting styles, and is straight for the square-cut garments. Its width is regulated solely by Fashion. For a double-breasted Paletot, it may vary from 2½, to 3, or even to 4 inches. For single-breasted styles, from 1½ to 2, or 2½ inches, is the most usual width, and some cutters give as little as 1 inch only, which however, we think is hardly sufficient.

VARIATIONS IN STYLE, &c.

(*Plate* 29.)

By the system of drawing the side seams of back and forepart, that we have just described, it will be seen that these seams must always be in accordance with each other, and the extra fulness allowed may be regulated to the greatest possible nicety; advantages which have never been possessed by any other method. The back may be cut of any width desired, and whatever this may be, the side seam of forepart will always agree with it.

Although however, by this principle Paletots may be cut with *any degree* of fulness, and with *any width* of back, yet we must here observe that there are certain proportions, between the width of back and the fulness of a garment, which are in better taste than others, and to which Fashion always returns, even when it has deviated from them for a time.

With the system here given, we could make a square-cut Paletot with a very narrow back, or a close-fitting Paletot with an extremely wide back

(Plate 29.)

without the fit of the garment being in any way deranged: but as in Architecture, there are certain fixed proportions for the various parts of a building; as in a Painting, there must be a certain harmony between the colors; as in Anatomy, there are certain regular proportions between all the parts of the body; so in our Profession, there are certain proportions between the various parts of a garment, which should not as a general rule, be deviated from.

For a CLOSE-FITTING PALETOT (fig. 1), about 4½ or 5 inches is the most elegant width at waist, and 1½ for the lowering of back scye.

For a MEDIUM STYLE (see figs. 1 and 2, *plate* 27), 6 or 6½ for the width at waist, and 2 for the extra depth of back scye, will be found the most harmonious proportion.

For a SQUARE-CUT PALETOT (see fig. 2, *plate* 29) the most suitable width at waist is about 8 inches, and the scye may be deepened any quantity preferred, but never less than 2½.

As a further guide to our readers, we here give a table of Waist Measures, showing in

(Plate 29.)

inches the width of back at waist most suitable in each size, for a medium-fitting Paletot.

For a Waist of	12½	{ the width of back at waist should be }	5 in.
,,	13¾	,,	5½ ,,
,,	15	,,	6 ,,
,,	16¼	,,	6½ ,,
,,	17½	,,	7 ,,
,,	18¾	,,	7½ ,,
,,	20	,,	8 ,,

For a close-fitting Paletot, the width of back *should not exceed this*, and for a square-cut one it *should never be less.*

Figs. 1 and 2 show two examples of the application of the principles we have just laid down. Fig. 1 is a close-fitting Paletot, for a proportionate structure, and fig. 2 is a square-cut Paletot, also for a proportionate structure. The backs in both patterns will be found to have the respective widths at waist and depths of back scye, that we have just mentioned, and with figs. 1 and 2, in *plate* 27, they form a complete series of Paletots for a proportionate man.

VARIATIONS IN THE CUT.

(*Plate* 29.)

Figs. 1 and 2 on this plate, also show a few slight variations from the draft as we have described it, which may be at times required.

HIGH OR LOW SHOULDERS. FIG. 1.

Fig. 1. If the slope measure has been taken and used in the draft, the pattern will of course be perfectly correct in this respect; but if not, and the client's shoulders are observed to be *very High* or *very Low*, it will be a good plan to vary the slope of this part, as shown on the diagram.

MORE OR LESS FULNESS IN THE SKIRT.

Fig. 1. Besides the extra fulness given at the waist of a Paletot, as explained on page 92, the *Skirt* may be cut so as to have more or less fulness at the bottom, as shown by the strong black line at the side seam, in this diagram. This extra width given to the skirt, should always be gradated to nothing, a little below the waist line.

FISH IN THE NECK SEAM. FIG. 1.

Some cutters, instead of taking out the fish at the neck in the usual place, prefer to take it about 3 or 4 inches back, or nearer the middle of neck, and indeed for some styles of Paletot, this change in the place of fish becomes almost a necessity.

Fig. 1 shows that wherever the fish may be placed, it should always have a width of $1\frac{1}{2}$, unless the shoulder-piece is straightened, or unless indeed, the large size of waist should enable us to reduce the size of fish, as explained for fig. 2, *plate* 30.

NECK SEAM WITHOUT FISH. FIG. 2.

Fig. 2. For some styles of Paletot, especially those intended always to be worn buttoned up to the neck, it becomes necessary to omit the fish in the neck altogether, as shown by the strong black line on this diagram, and to compensate for the absence of this fish, the shoulder-piece must be straightened $1\frac{1}{4}$, because if this was not done, the front edge would droop or fall away.

(*Plate* 29.)

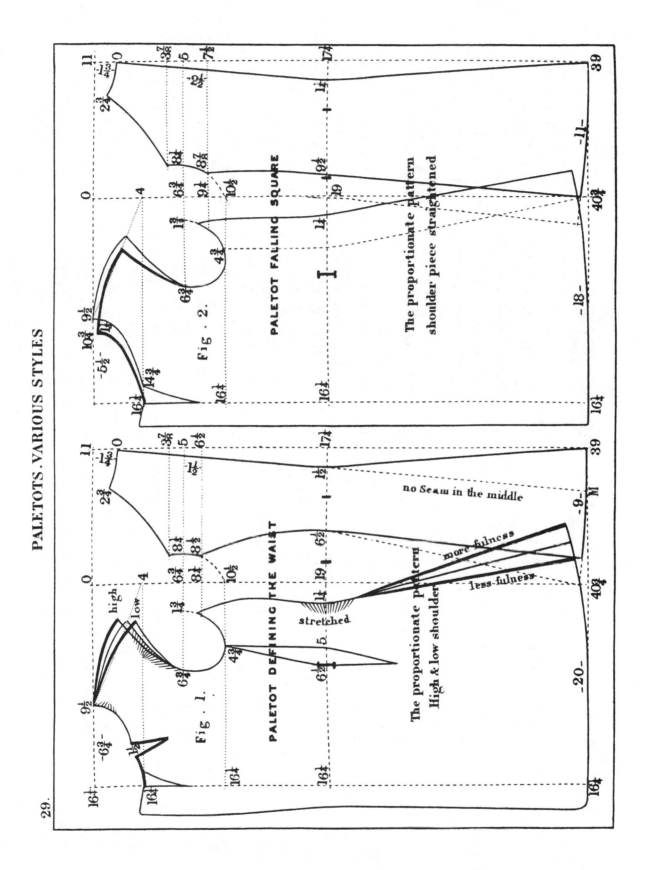

PALETOTS. VARIOUS STYLES

Fig. 1.

PALETOT DEFINING THE WAIST

The proportionate pattern
High & low shoulder

no Seam in the middle

more fulness

less fulness

stretched

high   low

Fig. 2.

PALETOT FALLING SQUARE

The proportionate pattern
shoulder piece straightened

29.

(*Plate* 29.)

In every case, however, in which a shoulder-piece is straightened, it ought at the same time to be shortened, for the reason explained in Part 1, page 31; the amount of shortening being more or less, according to the degree of straightening. The knowledge and application of this fact, will save much difficulty, and perhaps alterations and misfits. When a coat falls away at the front edge, the defect may in about two cases out of three, be traced to this cause, or to the neck seam being too long. It is a very common practice to reduce the size of fish in the neck, so as to render the making up more simple, and hitherto this has often been done, without even straightening the shoulder-piece at all, and in most cases without ever thinking of shortening it, or suspecting for an instant that a little change in the size of fish, might derange the balance of the garment.

BACK WITHOUT SEAM IN THE MIDDLE.

Fig. 1. For the close-fitting Paletot, we simply draw the middle of back, as a continuation of the sloping line from 0 to 1½; that is to say,

(*Plate* 29.)

continuing this line to the bottom at M, as shown by the long dotted line. The pattern should therefore for this style always be cut out on paper before laying it on the cloth. Of course the bottom of back skirt must be widened at the side seam, to compensate for the loss produced at the middle, but as it is bad to have the side seam of back too much curved, it is the best plan to give a little less width to the back, and more to the forepart, at the bottom of side seam. We do not, however, advise our readers to cut this style of Paletot without a seam in the middle, because it is rather difficult to make it up so as to have a good effect.

Fig. 2. For a square-cut Paletot also, the back may be without seam, the construction line being placed on the fold of cloth, and the usual hollow of back being omitted, so as to give more fulness at this part.

MAKING UP. FIGS. 1 & 2.

In making up a Paletot, the same principles must be followed, that have been already explained for coats. A little stretching should

(*Plate 29.*)

be given just above the front of scye, to give case to the arm; and to balance this stretching, the neck seam may be stretched a very little, at the curve just below the shoulder point. The greatest possible care, however, must be taken, *not to stretch the remaining part of neck*, and even to prevent it from stretching in making up.

In Paletots (see fig. 1) the side seam of forepart generally requires stretching at the hollow part of the waist, so as to distribute the fulness round the hip: the exact place is indicated by the shaded lines on the diagram. The quantity of stretching required, is in proportion to the amount the side seam is hollowed in at waist. For the closer-fitting styles, a good deal of stretching will be required, a less degree for medium styles, and square-cut Paletots, like fig. 2, require the side seam hardly stretched at all. Indeed, when THE SIDE SEAM is placed UNDER THE ARM, as shown by the long dotted lines, this seam, both in back and forepart, should be made up perfectly fair, without any stretching or fulling whatever.

LOOSE PALETOTS.

(*Plate 30.*)

The draft of loose Paletots is formed on the same principles that we have described for other Paletots, with the addition of certain extra allowances, to make the garment fit easier. The square which contains the back, must have more width (say for instance 15 or 16 inches or more), on account of the extra fulness at the bottom.

In the Forepart, the only differences from the ordinary draft are:—that though the shoulder-piece is always straightened, so as to avoid taking out a fish in the neck, yet for this style it is not shortened, as was explained for fig. 2, *plate* 29. The shortening is omitted, because a loose Paletot requires more ease in the arm-hole, and consequently greater length for the shoulder-strap.

The BACK in a loose Paletot is to be cut $\frac{3}{8}$ wider in every part, so that the back neck is marked at $3\frac{1}{8}$; the width of back stretch must be at $8\frac{5}{8}$ instead of $8\frac{1}{4}$; and the extreme

(Plate 30.)

width at the bottom of back scye, is at $11\frac{3}{8}$ instead of 11 as for an ordinary Paletot. Besides this the top part of back, including the back neck and the shoulder seam, must be drawn $\frac{1}{2}$ an inch higher up in the square than for other Paletots, so as to preserve the balance of the pattern, and compensate for the extra length given to the shoulder-piece of the forepart, by straightening it as we have just described.

The *Waist* measure in a Loose Paletot, need only be marked at the front part, unless in the case of *extremely* Stout Waists, because there will generally be quite sufficient fulness at the back, to allow of any ordinary increase of size.

DRAFT TO MEASURE.

Fig. 1 shows the Draft to Measure, which we think hardly needs any explanation, after the minute directions we have already given as to the draft for Paletots. We will however very briefly repeat our former instructions, at the same time combining with them the special changes required for the loose Overcoats.

(Plate 30..)

Form as usual the squares or compartments, the one for the forepart always being $16\frac{1}{4}$ wide, and the one for the back having a width of from 14 to 18 graduated inches, according to the fulness of the garment at the bottom. Then mark the *Balance*, the *Length*, and the *Side* to measure, as for a Paletot, and draw all the square lines across as usual.

For the *Back*:—First, mark the height of back neck at $\frac{1}{2}$ an inch higher than its usual place in a Paletot, and rule the width at $3\frac{1}{8}$, making it curve $\frac{3}{4}$ upwards, instead of $\frac{5}{8}$ as for a Paletot. Next mark the width of back stretch at $8\frac{5}{8}$, and of the bottom of back scye at $11\frac{3}{8}$. The curves are all drawn as usual, except that the height of back scye above the square line, is $1\frac{1}{2}$, instead of $1\frac{1}{8}$ as usual, and the middle of back is always drawn on the construction line, to give extra fulness at waist.

In the *Forepart*, all the fixed points are ruled exactly the same as for a Paletot, except that the *straightening* of the shoulder point, is at $10\frac{3}{4}$ from the construction line. The place

O

(Plate 30.)

of the front edge, is ruled by applying 1 more than half the waist measure, from the middle at 6½, and the back part of waist as usual.

To draw the side seam of the forepart, take the bottom of scye at 4¾, as a starting point, and add beyond this, 2 graduated inches for the place of side point: then spring out at the bottom, any quantity beyond the construction line, according to the fulness required; and draw the seam in a straight line from top to bottom.

For the side seam of Back, take the extreme width of back scye as a starting point, and take off 1¼ graduated inches or less for the width, to compensate for the extra allowance in the forepart, and draw the side seam to Fashion or to taste : for a very loose Paletot the width may be left at 11⅜, so that there will be an extra fulness of 2 graduated inches under the arm, and then a corresponding degree of fulness should be given at the bottom, as shown by the long dotted lines. This extra fulness of 2 inches under the arm, is the greatest degree of looseness that we think it is advisable

(Plate 30.)

to give to a Loose Paletot. If more fulness is required, the place of the shoulder seam should be altered, so as to come exactly on the top of shoulder ; the garment is then usually called a Sleeved Cloak or Paletot Sac, and the manner of drafting it is entirely changed (see *plate* 32).

Box Coats for Coachmen, are usually cut like the loosest style shown on fig. 1, with the addition of from 5 to 7 capes, cut as explained on *plate* 34. Full instructions as to the making up of Box Coats are given in " DEVERE'S MODERN BRITISH LIVERIES," which is especially devoted to this branch of the profession.

VARIATIONS FOR STOUT WAISTS.
FIG. 2.

In all the diagrams of Paletots that we have just described, it will be observed that the front edge is drawn parallel to the construction line. There is however, one important exception to this general rule :—we refer to Paletots for VERY STOUT WAISTED MEN.

In these exceptional sizes, the waist line springs out beyond the outside line of square,

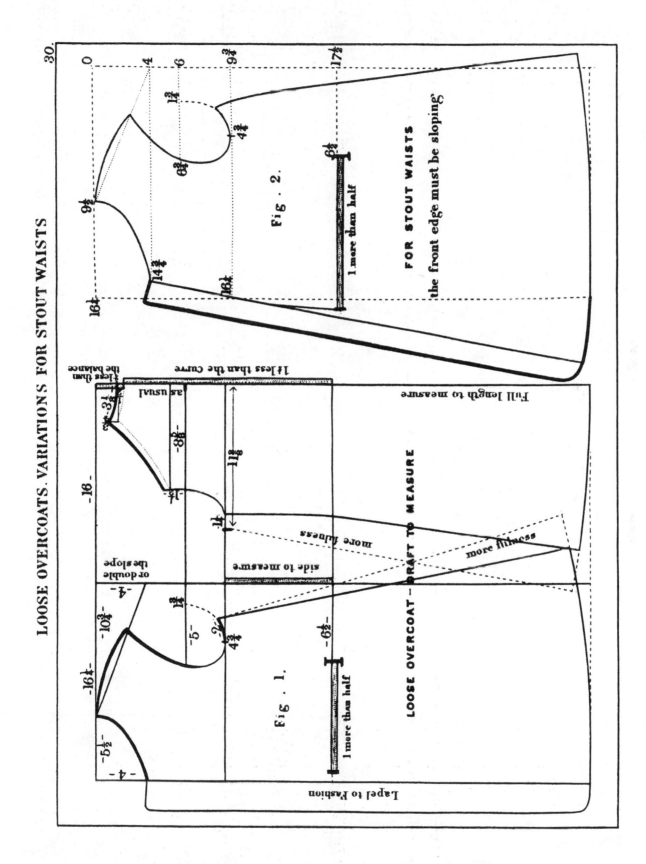

LOOSE OVERCOATS. VARIATIONS FOR STOUT WAISTS

Fig . 2.

FOR STOUT WAISTS
the front edge must be sloping

1 more than half

Fig . 1.

LOOSE OVERCOAT — DRAFT TO MEASURE

1 more than half

Lapel to Fashion

or double the slope

side to measure

more fullness

more fitness

Full length to measure

1½ less than the curve

as usual

less than the balance

(Plate .30)

as shown by fig. 2, and this of course renders it necessary to cut the front edge sloping, so as to give sufficient fulness to envelope the prominence of the stomach.

The waist being always marked from the middle point, will of course in every case indicate whether the front edge requires sloping or not, and the degree of springing out that should be given.

We must here call attention to one important result of this sloping of front edge; it will always reduce the size of the fish at the neck, more or less according to the degree of slope, and for extremely stout waists it will even do away with this fish altogether, as shown on the diagram, without requiring the shoulder-piece to be straightened, as would be the case for an ordinary size of waist.

For ordinary waists indeed, the front edge *might* be drawn sloping, if extra fulness is required at this part, but we do not think too much extra fulness at front would be at all desirable, even for Loose Paletots.

PALETOT JACKETS.

(Plate 31.)

The Paletot Jacket is a style of coat, which is in great demand for Lounging or Morning Costume, and for Country wear: it is cut without seam at waist, and like the Paletot, may be of every degree of fulness.

These elegant and convenient garments, are cut in precisely the same way as Paletots, except that the fronts are only 16 wide instead of 16¼: all the remarks that we have made in our explanation of the system for Paletots, apply equally to Paletot Jackets. The skirts are of course always cut shorter than for Overcoats.

In order to show our readers that there is no special difference in the draft of Paletot Jackets, except the width of the front square being ruled at 16 only, we have given on fig. 1 a Close Fitting Jacket, and on fig. 2 a Square Cut Style.

We will not again repeat all our former instructions as to the DRAFT TO MEASURE, which the diagrams themselves will be found suffi-

(Plate 31.)

ciently to explain, but we will give a few re-marks on the cut of each style, most of which we may observe will apply to Paletots of all kinds, as well as to Paletot Jackets.

CLOSE-FITTING STYLE. FIG. 1.

This style of Jacket is usually made single-breasted: the lapel having a width of 1½ at the top and breast line, the skirt being gradually cut away, or falling square according to Fashion. The back has a width at waist of 4¾, and the extra depth of back scye is 1 only.

It is often desirable for this style, to reduce the size of fish in the neck;—to do this—straighten the shoulder-piece ½ an inch (to 10), and also shorten it a little, thus reducing the width required for the fish to 1 inch.

The strong black line on this diagram, shows a new and improved method of cutting the side body, in a close-fitting Paletot or Paletot Jacket. In fig. 1, *plate* 29, the fish under the arm was cut with both sides equally curved, and the side seam of forepart requires stretch-ing at the hollow of waist. Now this stretch-

(Plate 31.)

ing, requires a good deal of care and skill on the part of the workman, and it may be avoided by cutting the side point and the bottom of scye in the side body, ¾ of an inch higher than its usual place; at the same time, drawing the seam of the fish next the side body, in a straight line, as shown by the black lines: this side of the fish will then be longer than the side next the forepart, and the forepart side will require about ⅜ of an inch stretching at the waist, so as to make the two sides of the fish of equal length. No stretching will then be required in the side seam at the waist; the fulness will thus be found equally distributed at the hips, and the Paletot will sit better at this part, with less trouble in the making up.

SQUARE-CUT PALETOT JACKET. FIG. 2.

This style is always in favor, sometimes it is made single-breasted, and forms a most convenient garment for Summer wear, especially for suits. Sometimes it is made double-breasted, and is a favorite jacket for Winter,

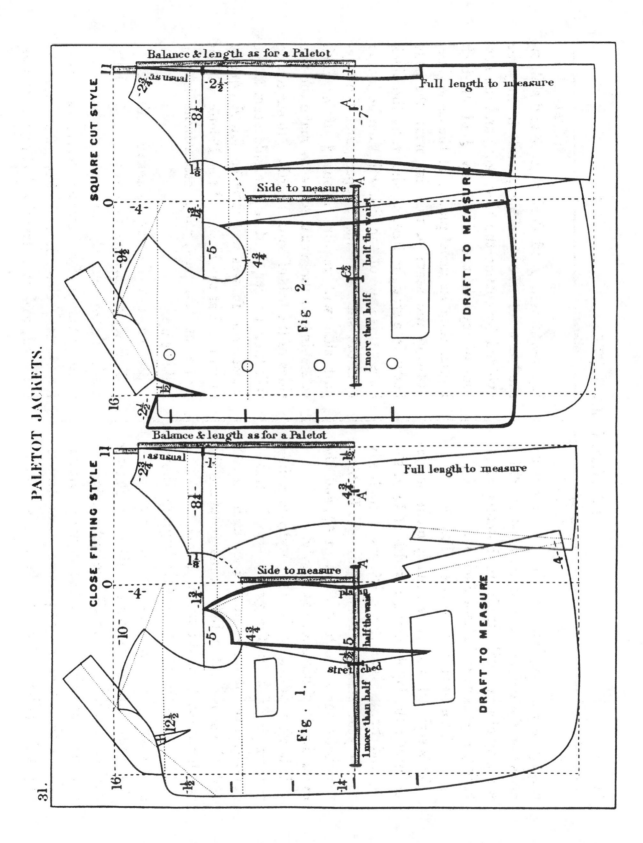

PALETOT JACKETS.

31.

(*Plate* 31.)

under the names of the Reefer or Pea Jacket; it is indicated by the strong black line. The width of back at waist is 7, the back scye being cut with an additional depth of 2½ inches. The side seams may either be drawn like the black lines, so as to define the waist in a slight degree, or they may be drawn quite straight as shown by the plain lines. The Pea Jackets generally have the skirts cut very short; for other styles the lengths very according to Fashion.

To fix the place for the buttons in a double-breasted Jacket or Paletot, draw first the buttonholes, and then mark inside the construction line, about 1 inch less than the width of lapel at the corresponding places : of course the top button must be placed further back than this, on account of the fish in the neck.

The back may either have a seam in the middle, with vent or opening left at the bottom, as indicated by the strong black line, or the middle of back may remain on the construction line so as to have no seam at this part, and the width of back will then of course be 8 instead of 7.

SLEEVED CLOAKS.

(*Plate* 32.)

This garment, which is also called a *Paletot-sac*, is a kind of Loose Paletot ; cut with even more fulness than those we have described, and having the shoulder seam placed on the top of of shoulder, instead of at the back.

This change in the place of the seam, though apparently of no importance, nevertheless causes a complete difference in the aspect of the garment, in the manner in which it hangs, and above all in the way of drafting it.

The great degree of fulness given to a Sleeved Cloak, enables us to render the draft much simpler, and the forepart and back may each be drafted at once on the cloth, because the construction line of forepart is placed at the front edge.

DRAFT TO MEASURE, FIGS. 1 & 2.

For the BACK, fig. 2 :—Draw first the construction line, and with a graduated measure corresponding to the breast measure of the client, form all the upper part of the pattern,

(*Plate* 32.)

as shown on the diagram, putting the same figures for all sizes and structures. Next rule the length of back to measure, or to Fashion, and mark upwards from the bottom, 2½ graduated inches for the slope of bottom edge.

Form the curve of bottom, giving it a width of 20 graduated inches for a medium degree of fulness, and complete the pattern by drawing the side seam in a straight line from top to bottom.

For the FOREPART, fig. 1 : Mark from the edge of cloth or paper, the width of lapel to Fashion, say from 2 to 4 inches, according as a single or double-breasted style is required. Then draw the construction line, and form all the top part of the pattern by the graduated measures. Rule the length of the front edge, at about 2¼ less than the middle of back ; or give from 0 to the bottom, the same length as that of the back, from 0 to the bottom of skirt.

Mark up 2½ graduated inches for the slope of the bottom edge, and make the width at bottom the same as that of the back, measuring from the construction line and not including

the lapel. The side seam is drawn in a straight line, and the bottom edge in a regular curve.

This Sleeved Cloak, cut with the skirt very long, and with the Sleeve fig. 3, gives the pattern of a DRESSING GOWN.

VARIATIONS IN STRUCTURE.

If we examine the changes required in a Sleeved Cloak, to suit the numerous variations of structure that are met with, we shall find that the fulness of the garment renders these changes very few in number.

Neither the size of the waist nor the length of the body are to be taken into account, because the coat is so very loose at the waist, that it will fit equally well at this part, whether the man is Thin or Stout, and whether the place of the natural waist is higher or lower. The large size of the scye also renders it unnecessary to take any account, either of the length of side, or the size of the shoulder.

The only changes required are for High and Low Shoulders, and for the Stooping or Extra-erect builds.

(*Plate* 32.)

PALETOT SACS OR SLEEVED CLOAKS.

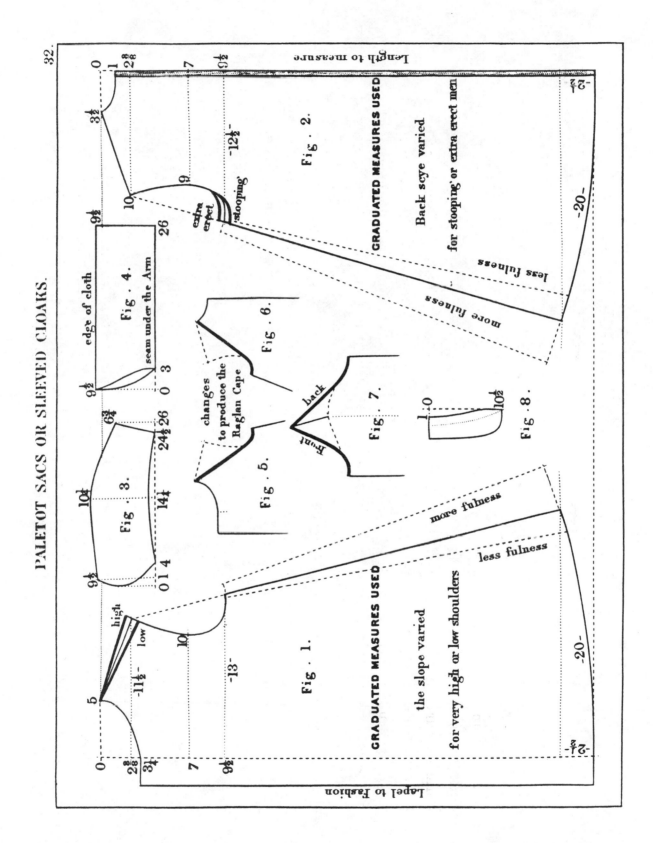

(*Plate 32.*)

Fig. 1.   For the shoulders these changes are made in the forepart only, as shown by the strong black lines.   For a high shoulder give *less Slope* to the shoulder seam, and for a low shoulder give *more Slope*; but rarely varying more than ¾ of an inch, from the proportionate structure.

Fig. 2.   For the Stooping and Extra-erect structures, the *bottom of scye* in the back must be *made higher or lower* so as to vary the balance.   For stooping men, the depth of scye, instead of being at 9½ down, may be increased to 10 or 10¼, and for extra-erect men, on the contrary, it may have a depth of 9 or 8¾ only. These are the extreme degrees of variation, and should never be exceeded : in most cases a very slight variation will be found sufficient.

VARIATIONS IN FULNESS.

The width at bottom that we have indicated on figs. 1 and 2 is the medium degree of fulness, and that which will be the oftenest required ; but more or less width may be given

(*Plate 32.*)

if preferred.   Of course the bottom edge, will be curved up more for the very full styles, and less for the narrower ones.

Another point to which we must call attention, is that for every 2 inches of increase at the bottom, a ¼ of an inch must be added at the top of side seam, so as to increase the size of the scye.   Again, if the bottom is cut narrower, a little less width may be given under the arm.

SLEEVES.

We have drafted these to a smaller size than the other pieces, so as to take less room on the plate.

Fig. 3 is the most usual form of Sleeve, which is drafted to measure in the same way as for an ordinary Paletot, except that it has a width of 9½ at the top to agree with the large size of armhole, and that less round is given to the sleeve head, on account of the great width of the shoulder-piece.

Fig. 4 is another style of Sleeve, suited for a Sleeved Cloak.   It has one seam only, which

(Plate 32.)

is placed underneath the arm, and will of course be of the same width from top to bottom.

THE RAGLAN CAPE.

This style of Sleeved Cloak, once so fashionable, has the seams of the sleeve running up to a point at the neck; the manner of drafting it is explained by figs. 5, 6, and 7.

Take first the pattern of a *Paletot-sac* of the ordinary form, with the sleeve cut like fig. 4, and opened out to its full width. Then cut off the corners from the shoulder-pieces of back and forepart, so as to have the shoulder seams running straight, from the shoulder point and back neck, to the bottom of scye (see the strong black lines on figs. 5 and 6). Then add these two corners at the top of sleeve, as shown by fig. 7, so that they form only one piece with the sleeve head.

The COLLAR for a Sleeved Cloak or *Paletot-sac*, may be cut like fig. 8, in this plate, or like figs. 4, 5, or 7 in *plate 34*

(Plate 33.)

INVERNESS CAPES.

One of the most convenient of all Cloaks, and the one which is in most general use, is the Inverness Cape. It is a kind of Cloak with large armhole, this armhole being covered by a cape, which is placed at the front part of the garment only. Its appearance is shown by fig. 6.

This Cape is most commodious and comfortable in wear, either for travelling, or as a wrapper for evening parties, or Theatres. It is so loose that it does not disarrange the costume worn underneath; and the large size of the armhole, permits it to be put on and taken off with the greatest possible facility. The cape affords that protection to the chest, required in this climate by a gentleman who is wearing a full evening dress costume.

The only measures required for an Inverness Cape, are the *Breast*; the *Full Length of Back*, from the neck to the bottom; and the *Length of Cape*, measured from the neck point of forepart, to the level of the knuckles or hand.

DRAFT TO MEASURE.

(*Plate* 33.)

The draft of the Inverness Cape, is formed in a very similar manner to what we have described for Sleeved Cloaks, except that in a loose Cape like this, we need not take any account whatever, of the variations in structure. The lengths are ruled to measure, and the fixed points are all marked by the graduated measures in the usual way.

The BACK, FIG. 3. Draw the construction line; mark on it 1 for the curve of back neck, and rule the full length to measure; form the upper part of the back, by a graduated measure nearest the breast measure of the client; give a slope of 3 inches for the bottom edge, mark the width of bottom at 24, and draw the curves by the hand.

The FRONT, fig. 1. Draw all the upper part of the pattern including the armhole, by the graduated measures; allow any width for the lapel, making the length of front edge 2½ less than the length of back: draw the bottom edge at 24 wide, and slope it up 2½ only.

(*Plate* 33.)

N.B. For very large sizes, 19 graduated inches will be too great a depth to give to the armhole. For these, this part may be ruled at a distance of from 0, equal to half the length of back.

The CAPE. fig. 2, may be cut of various degrees of width. The strong black line shows the degree of fulness, which is we think, best suited for general adoption: a good deal more fulness might be given (see the line 4, 5, 35), and this style has we think, a very handsome effect, besides giving very great ease for the motions of the arm. The *least degree of fulness that should ever be given* to the cape, is that shown on our diagram—27 inches wide at bottom, and we do not recommend this width, as it will slightly confine the motions of the arm : some tailors however prefer it, on account of its taking less material.

The neck seam of cape is to be drafted by the graduated measures : the front length must be ruled to measure, and the bottom edge swept from the star at 5. To find the width

(Plate 33.)

for a *medium style of cape*, draw a line square across, at a distance from 0, of half the length between 0 and the bottom of front edge. For a *Narrow Cape*, mark a width of 27 graduated inches at bottom, and for *a very Full Cape* take the line at the top, which is drawn square with the construction line. Point 35 of the wide Cape, and 31 of the medium Cape, are intended to show the general or average depth to which the Cape should be cut, and which may serve as a guide when the measure of the front length of Cape has not been taken.

It will be observed that in the Cape, the depth of the neck point from 0, is 3; while in the front it is 3½; all the other figures of neck and shoulder being exactly the same for both pieces. The reason of this is: that as the cape in addition to laying over the front, has also to cover the thickness of the arm, more fulness is required, which is here obtained by shortening the neck seam. If this was not done, the cape would fall away at the front edge.

(Plate 33.)

For the COLLAR, either fig. 4 or fig. 5 will do equally well. Fig. 4 is that used by most cutters, but we rather give the preference to fig. 5, as it is so well suited to wear turned down all round, as shown by fig. 6.

MAKING UP.

The manner of joining these pieces together is very simple and easy. The front (fig. 1) is joined to the back (fig. 3) at the shoulder seam and bottom of side seam only; leaving the part of the front which is hollowed out, as an opening to pass the arm through: this opening is covered by the cape (fig. 2) which is sewn to the neck of the forepart, and to the side seam of the back from the top as far as it will reach.

The best materials for these capes are:—For Evening Wrappers or the Theatres: dark colored Meltons or Waterproof Cloths of good substance and quality. (A most simple and effective receipt for waterproofing will be found in our Supplementary Part.) For general Winter Wear or for Travelling, we recommend stout Pilots, Witneys, or fancy diagonals; the

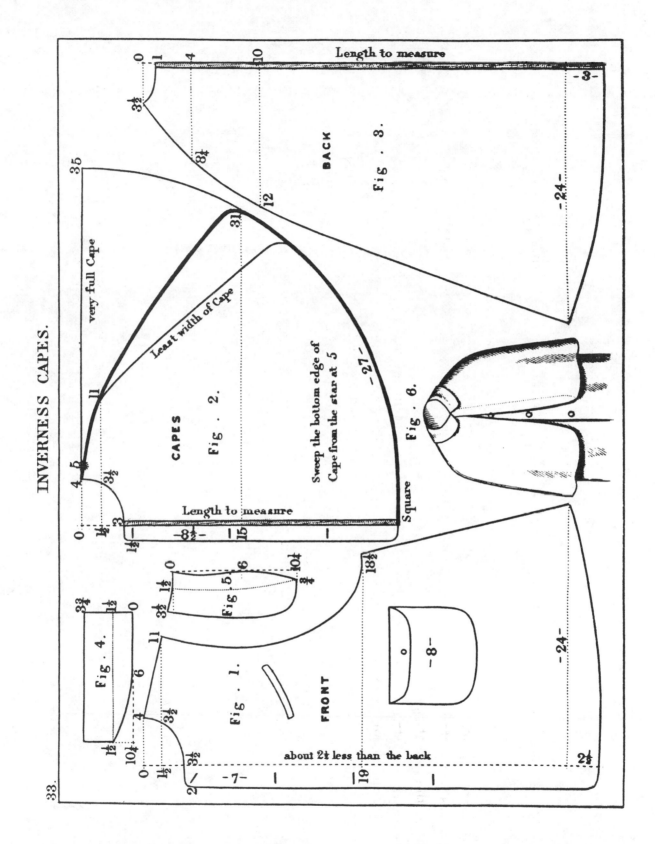

INVERNESS CAPES.

Length to measure

BACK

Fig . 3.

−3−

−24−

very full Cape

Least width of Cape

CAPES

Fig . 2.

Sweep the bottom edge of
Cape from the star at 5

−27−

Fig . 6.

Square

Length to measure

−8½−

about 2¼ less than the back

Fig . 5.

Fig . 4.

Fig . 1.

FRONT

−8−

−24−

−7−

−19−

2½

33.

(*Plate 33.*)

edges bound with braid, and the collars covered with velvet to match. For Summer or Tourists' wear, and for the Races, Light Waterproof Tweed is the best material. If linings are required, Alpaca is the most appropriate.

The fronts are generally made single-breasted, having a width of about 2 for the lapel: they close by four buttons and buttonholes, 7 inches apart: in addition to the buttons, there should be a large hook and eye at top. The Cape has the lapel about half an inch less in width than the front, it closes by a fly, and the three buttons are placed 8½ inches apart, so that they may not come exactly over the buttons of the fronts.

The pockets in the front skirts, should be about 8 inches wide, stitched on outside: they should be covered by small flaps fastening by buttons, so as to prevent anything from falling out if the coat is taken off and laid on one side, as at the Theatre, or in travelling, &c. For Travelling or for Tourists, an additional outside breast pocket on the left side, will be found most convenient and serviceable.

CLOAKS AND CAPES.

(*Plate 34.*)

Cloaks and Capes are garments which are but rarely made at the present time. We have however given the principal styles, and those which are most likely to be required. We have here greatly simplified the draft of all styles, by giving for each a central point or pivot, from which the bottom edge may be swept or cast; thus avoiding all measurement and calculation.

SPANISH OR CIRCULAR CLOAK. FIG. 1.

For this form, the front edge is placed the right way of the stuff, and the back the wrong way. It is usually cut to reach nearly to the ankles, so that there will be a seam in the middle of back, on account of the width of cloth.

The Draft is very easy. Form the neck by the graduated measures; then mark the length of back to measure, and draw the bottom edge square with the middle of back for about 3½ inches; from this place sweep the bottom edge (the star in the middle of neck at 3½ is

(*Plate* 34.)

the pivot) to about 4 inches from the construction line of front, from which place the bottom is drawn square with the construction line.

This style of Cloak is sometimes made to fasten by hook and eye at the top. If it is to button, any width may be added for the lapel.

The Cape Collar (fig. 6) is best suited for this cloak; it has no stand, and falls flat all round the shoulders: if a collar with stand is required, fig. 7 is the most suitable.

Half Circle Cloak. Fig. 2.

This style of Cloak is rarely required except for ladies. It is not as graceful as either fig. 1 or 3, but it has one advantage, that of taking less stuff. The neck is marked as it is by graduated measures, and the length of back ruled to measure. Then draw the bottom edge square from the back for 3 or 4 inches, and taking the star as a centre, sweep the bottom to about 6 or 7 inches from the front, from which place it is drawn square with the construction line. The Collars, figs. 4, 6, or 7, would either be suited to this Cloak.

(*Plate* 34.)

Three-quarter Circle. Fig. 3.

This is perhaps the best form of cloak that can be made. It sits perfectly smooth on the shoulders, and the folds fall naturally and gracefully. The draft is the same as for the other styles of cloak. Form the neck by the graduated measures : rule the length of back as required, and draw the bottom square with the middle of back for a few inches ; from the pivot or star, sweep the bottom to within 4 or 5 inches of the construction line of front, and complete it so as to be square with the front edge. The width of lapel is ruled to Fashion or to taste. Any of the collars on this plate will suit this cloak.

Capes. Fig. 3.

These are drafted exactly in the same way as the Three Quarter Circle Cloak, but of course are cut much shorter. For a Coachman's Box Coat, measure the length of the deepest cape at back, and decrease them regularly all round as shown on the diagram.

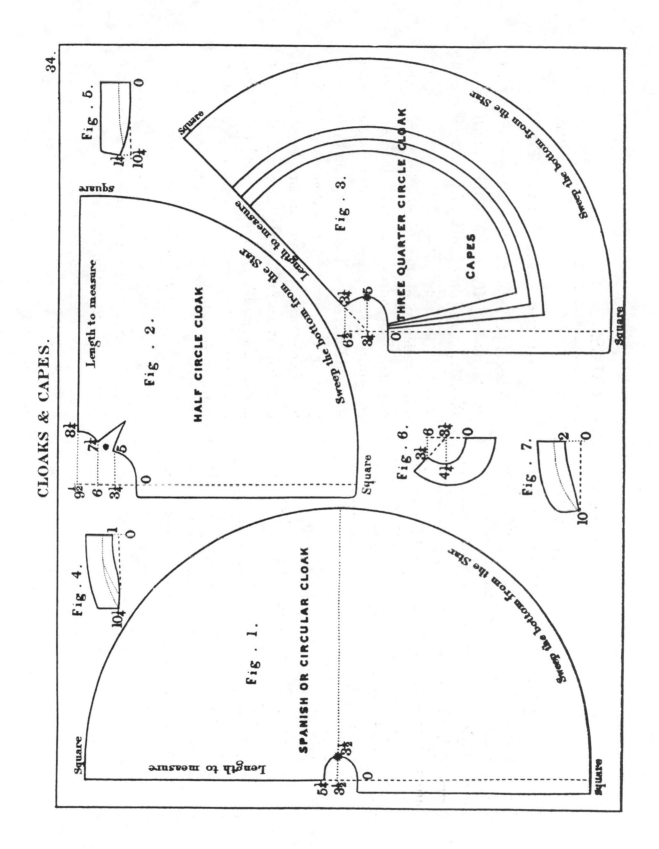

CLOAKS & CAPES.

34.

Fig. 5.

Fig. 2.

Length to measure

HALF CIRCLE CLOAK

THREE QUARTER CIRCLE CLOAK

CAPES

Fig. 3.

Sweep the bottom from the Star

Length to measure

Sweep the bottom from the Star

square

Square

Fig. 6.

Fig. 7.

Fig. 4.

Fig. 1.

SPANISH OR CIRCULAR CLOAK

Length to measure

Square

Square

Sweep the bottom from the Star

(*Plate* 34.)

The COLLARS on this plate, figs. 4, 5, 6, and 7, show all the styles that are used for cloaks.

Fig. 4, is suited for cloaks that are to be worn either buttoned up or turned back.

Fig. 5, is similar to the collar of a coat, and by a little care in working, will suit any style.

Fig. 6 is a Cape Collar ; that is to say, it has no stand whatever, and is only suited for the Spanish Cloak, or for Ladies.

Fig. 7, is a regular Cloak Collar, to be worn turned down all round.

LADIES' PALETOTS AND SLEEVED MANTLES.

(*Plate* 35).

The making up of Ladies' Mantles, and tight-fitting Jackets or Paletots for outdoor wear, is a department of the Profession, which was almost unknown in this country, until we called the attention of our Subscribers to its advantages, and to the extension of business that might be obtained, by cultivating this branch of the Tailor's Art. Cloth of various

(*Plate* 35.)

styles, forms the most appropriate material, and some woollen-drapers now make this department a special feature of their business.

We have given in this work, systems for drafting the three principal forms, now worn by ladies ; and which in themselves, will be found to include all styles. With a few slight and unimportant modifications, or changes in the place of seams, they will apply to any new forms, that may hereafter become fashionable.

MEASUREMENT.

The measures to take are only five in number :—

No. 1. *Breast ;* taken on the dress as for a Riding Habit, and indicating the graduated measure to use in forming the draft.

No. 2. *Waist ;* taken on the dress, and moderately tight. The proportionate waist gives usually, about 4 or 5 graduated inches less than the breast.

No. 3. *Length of Back* to natural waist; which point is easily ascertained in a lady, on account of the fulness of the petticoats.

(*Plate* 35.)

No. 4. *Full Length*; from back neck to bottom of skirt.

No. 5. *Length of Sleeve*; from the middle seam of back to the wrist as usual.

To these may be added the *Size round the Skirt* of the dress, at the level of the full length required; measured rather loose, and with about 6 inches added for extra fulness. Like the *Breast* and *Waist*, it is written down as half. This width is usually distributed as follows :—

In a Tight-fitting or Medium Paletot: Three-eighths to the front, three-eighths to the side-piece, and a fourth to the back.

For a Loose Paletot: Half to the front, and half to the back.

CLOSE-FITTING PALETOT.

(*Plate* 35.)

The black lines on figs. 1, 2, and 3, show a Lady's Paletot, which is cut so as to fit as close to the waist as possible. It consists of back, side-piece, and front or forepart, and these pieces ought strictly speaking, to be drafted in three

squares, in a similar way to that already described for coats. As however, it rarely happens that a cutter has a sheet of paper or even a table, large enough to do this, we will explain how to draft each piece one after the other, commencing with :—

THE BACK, fig. 3. Draw the construction line, and mark on it, first, $1\frac{1}{8}$ for the slope of back neck, then the length of back to measure, and also the full length to the bottom of skirt.

Next mark the regular depth of back scye, at $1\frac{1}{4}$ less than half the length of back, and give $2\frac{1}{2}$ above this for the top of back scye. Rule the widths as shown on the diagram, by the graduated measures. Mark the width of bottom to Fashion or measure, and rise up about 2 for the slope of bottom edge. All the curves are drawn by the hand.

For the FRONT, fig. 1. The back being cut out, lay it on a sheet of paper, and then mark on the edge of the paper at the level of the back stretch, and $2\frac{3}{4}$ below it for the depth of scye; next mark at the waist; and at $2\frac{1}{2}$ less

(*Plate* 35.)

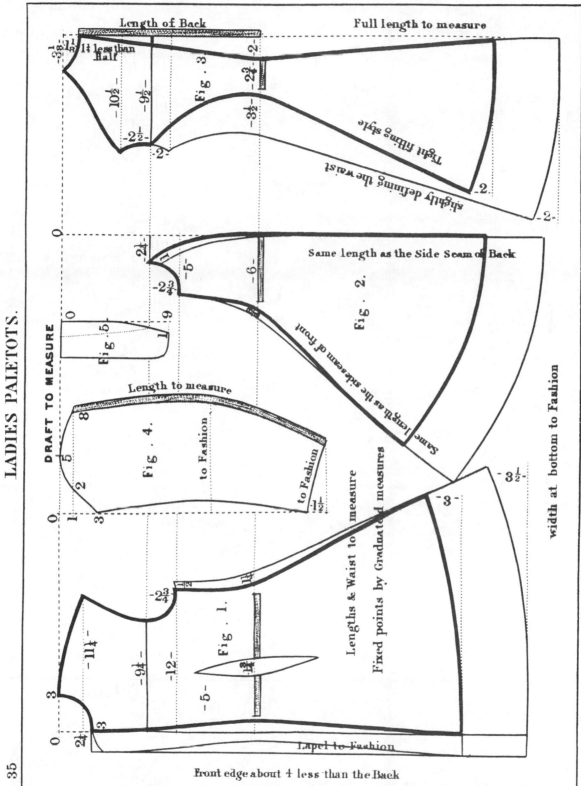

LADIES PALETOTS.

Length of Back

Full length to measure

Fig . 3

Tight fitting style

slightly defining the waist

DRAFT TO MEASURE

Same length as the Side Seam of Back

Fig . 2.

Same length as the side-seam of front

Fig . 5

Length to measure

to Fashion

Fig . 4.

to Fashion

Lengths & Waist to measure

Fixed points by Graduated measures

Fig . 1.

width at bottom to Fashion

Lapel to Fashion

Front edge about ¼ less than the Back

35

(*Plate* 35.)

than the length of back, to give the length of front. Draw lines square across.

Complete the top part of the pattern with the graduated measures.

Then slope the front edge at waist; take out the fish in the waist; and regulate the size of waist according to the measure, of course deducting that part of the measure which is given in the back and side body. Rise up about **3** graduated inches for the slope of the bottom, and mark the width of bottom to Fashion or to measure.

The Side-piece, fig. 2. Take the back, lay it on another sheet of paper, and mark on the edge, at the height of back stretch, and at the waist line : then mark downward 2¾ graduated inches from the first mark, to find the depth of scye, and draw lines square across.

Then on the top line mark in 2¼ graduated inches : at the second, mark 5 graduated inches; and at the waist, about 6 graduated inches, or a little more or less than this, if the waist is larger or smaller than the regular proportion.

(*Plate* 35.)

Rule the length of side seam to agree with the back; and the length of the seam under the arm, to agree with the front, and mark the width of bottom to measure or to Fashion, starting from the construction line.

Sleeves are drafted in the usual way.

Collars may be drawn by the graduated measures, for all sizes and styles. Those given in *plate* 36 will suit this Paletot.

Lapels. Any width may be added beyond the construction line, if the Paletot is to fasten by buttons. If to hook and eye, as is most usual, the construction line gives the right place of front edge.

PALETOT SLIGHTLY MARKING THE WAIST.

This style is shown by the plain lines of figs. 1, 2, and 3. It is drafted just the same as the tight-fitting styles, except that the back is cut wider at waist, and 2 graduated inches deeper at back scye, only 1 being taken off at the top of side to compensate for it; so that an extra fulness is left at this part. Besides

(*Plate 35.*)

this, a little extra fulness may be allowed at the seam under the arm, both of back and fore-part, as shown on the diagram.

LADIES' SLEEVED MANTLES.

(*Plate 36.*)

These are sometimes called Loose Paletots, or Sleeved Cloaks. The draft is extremely simple, and is shown by figs, 1 and 2.

The BACK, fig. 2. Form the upper part of back by the graduated measures. Rule the length to measure ; draw a line square from this for about 4 inches, and sweep the bottom from the pivot at $3\frac{1}{8}$, making the width according to Fashion or to measure.

For the FOREPART, fig. 1. Form the upper part by the graduated measures ; make the length of side seam and the width of bottom equal to those of the back, and sweep the bottom from the star or pivot at $2\frac{3}{4}$ on the shoulder seam. A lapel must be added if the fronts are to button.

The SLEEVE (fig. 3) is drawn in the usual way.

(*Plate 36.*)

Fig. 4 gives the *Cape Collar*, which has no stand whatever.

Fig. 5 is a *Collar with Stand and Fall*, to be turned down all round.

The *Stand-up Collar* is cut like that of a Uniform, but not so deep.

Fig. 5, in *plate* 35, is an *Ordinary Collar*, to be used if the Paletot has a lapel and turnover like a coat.

We will conclude by a few remarks on Making these garments.

The materials in general use, are Fancy Cloths of all kinds, Vicunas, Astracan, Seal Skins, Velvets, &c.: fresh novelties are brought out every season. For linings, Silk looks the best, but Alpaca is the most durable.

In the style and kind of Trimmings, there is an almost endless variety. Velvet is much used, and so are fancy Silk Braids of rich design. *Passementerie* and Gimp trimmings, are usually sold in sets by drapers or trimming-makers.

36

LADIES LOOSE PALETOTS OR SLEEVED CLOAKS.

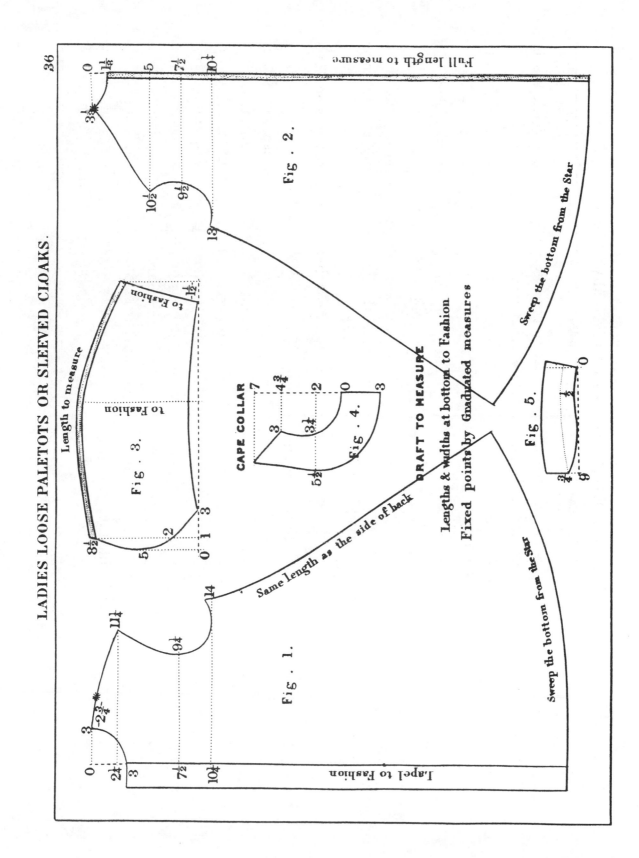

Full length to measure

Fig . 2.

Sweep the bottom from the Star

0
1¼
5
7½
10¼
3⅜

10½
9½

13

Length to measure

to Fashion

to Fashion

Fig . 3.

1½
8½
5
2
0 1 3

CAPE COLLAR

7
4¾
3
3¼
2
0
5½
3

Fig . 4.

DRAFT TO MEASURE

Lengths & widths at bottom to Fashion
Fixed points by Graduated measures

Same length as the side of back

Fig . 5.

0
¼
¾
9

Sweep the bottom from the Star

14

11¼
2¾
9¼

3

0
2¼
3
7½
10¼

Lapel to Fashion

Fig . 1.

Sweep the bottom from the Star

DEVERE'S

HANDBOOK OF PRACTICAL CUTTING.

PART THE FOURTH.

In the first parts of this work, we have thoroughly explained the true theory of the Art of Cutting, based on accurate and infallible principles for all kinds of garments, and have explained an easy and simple system of measurement, which in its direct application to the draft, provides for all the variations of structure that are met with in the human body. All these structures will be found most elaborately described in the "Tailor's Guide," and are there illustrated by drawings of the various figures, as well as by diagrams of the patterns suited for them, and of their differences from the proportionate structure. There are however some other matters, a knowledge of which is absolutely necessary for the head of an establishment, and is especially requisite for those about to commence business, and these form the subject of the present part of the Work.

Among these we may name: the Art of Placing Garments on the Cloth, with the greatest economy: the correct theory of Misfits, and how to avoid and correct them: a knowledge of the series of patterns most useful for ready-made Garments, and of the structure most often met with for each size.

To these we shall add instructions for working our System by the common inch tape only, which may be useful in case the graduated measures are mislaid, and shall conclude our work by a few hints on Capital, Interest, Credit, Selection of Stock, &c., which we think will be found well worthy the attention of our readers.

ECONOMY OF CLOTH.

(Plates 37 and 38.)

In placing a garment on the cloth two things have to be borne in mind; firstly, to use the least possible quantity of material, without contracting or cramping any of the pieces; and secondly, to have all the pieces placed on the cloth in their proper direction, that is to say,—having the construction lines on the straight thread of the cloth, or as nearly so as possible; if this is not attended to, the various parts of the pattern will not have the proper biais, the garment will hang ungracefully, and get out of shape after a little wear.

The plans or schemes here given, are for the medium sizes namely, from 17¾ to 19 breast; they are so arranged that the garments may, with a little care, be drafted at once upon the cloth, if this plan is preferred.

We must however, strongly recommend our readers always to cut out the pattern in paper, before marking it on the cloth. This method will be found far more accurate (unless the cutter has had a very lengthened experience), and it will be a great saving in material, and in the end will take less time. Another advantage is that the client's pattern can always be preserved, so as to avoid the necessity of cutting a fresh pattern for each order, as would be the case if the garment was chalked at once on the cloth.

The widths of cloth that we have taken, are those in most general use; if wider or narrower cloths are used, our readers must of course vary the placing, according to their judgment.

WIDTHS OF ENGLISH CLOTHS.

(Plates 37 and 38.)

We have given a list of the cloths in most general use, with their average width in inches when thoroughly shrunk.

	WIDTH.
Black Cloths; medium and good qualities	60 inches.
Black Cloths; extra fine; 16s. to 21s. per yard	62 "
Black Cloths; common; under 8s.	54 "
Fancy Coating; good qualities ..	54 to 56

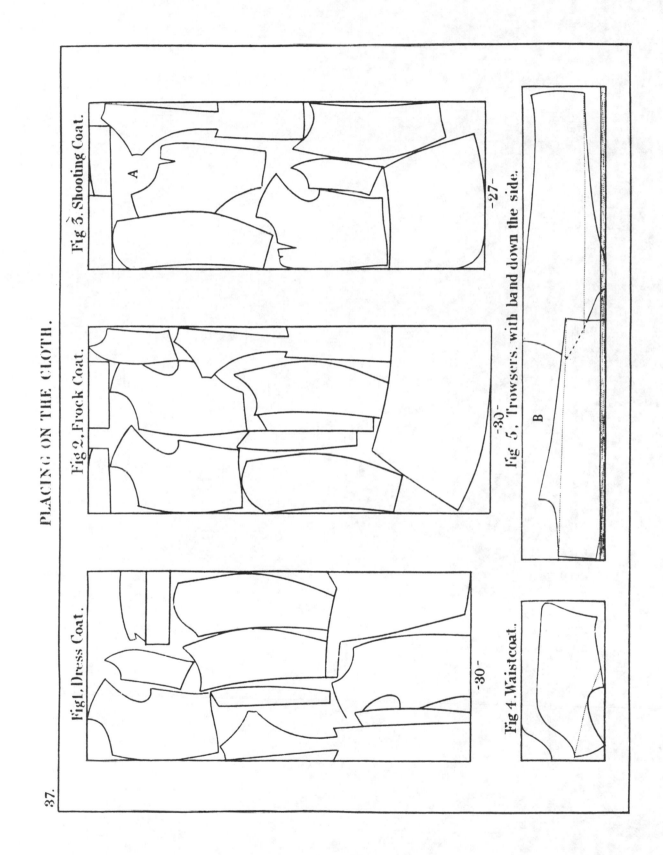

PLACING ON THE CLOTH.

Fig 1, Dress Coat.

Fig 2, Frock Coat.

Fig 3, Shooting Coat.

Fig 4, Waistcoat.

Fig 5, Trowsers, with band down the side.

A

B

-30-

-30-

-27-

37.

(*Plates 37 and 38.*)

Fancy Coatings ; best quality	..	58 inches.
Do. common	..	52 ,,
Meltons and Beavers ; about	..	60 ,,
Witney, Elysian, Pilot, Boxcloth, and most heavy goods	..	54 ,,
Trowserings ; black Doeskins, medium	.. ..	27 ,,
Trowserings ; black Doeskins, best		28 ,,
Scotch Angola and Platt's Tweeds		28 ,,

(or 27½ with both lists off)

Bordered Goods ; inside the borders		27½ ,,
Waistcoatings	.. ..	27 ,,
Silk..	.. ..	18 ,,
Velvets	.. ..	22 ,,
Moires	.. ..	24 ,,

(*Plate 37.*)

Fig. 1.—Dress Coat, placed on 60-inch cloth, folded in the centre as usual. When the length of back and skirt is 39 inches, it takes about 62 inches of cloth.

Fig. 2.—Frock Coat, placed on 60-inch cloth, takes about 65 inches of cloth, for a full length of 35.

(*Plate 37.*)

Fig. 3.—Shooting Coat on 54-inch cloth : this way of placing will also do for a Jacket or an Oxonian Coat. When pocket-flaps are required, they can be cut out of the space marked A, by piecing the shoulder-piece of front lining. For a full length of 33, about 64 inches of cloth will be required.

Fig. 4.—Waistcoat of the straight form without collar ; on a 27-inch material, folded.

Fig. 5.—Trowsers, with band at the side. This is a most convenient way of cutting, and will indeed do for any style of trowsers. Rather large pieces have to be joined in at the seat and top of back, but these will of course be hidden by the coat. The quantity of cloth required, is exactly double the length of side seam. When the piece marked B is opened out to its full width, the front of a waistcoat may be cut from it, by joining on corners at the shoulder-piece and at the bottom of scye, as shown by the fine dotted line on fig. 4 ; by this means one waistcoat may be cut out, from every two pairs of trowsers.

(Plate 38.)

Fig. 1.—PALETOT, on a 54-inch Pilot or similar material. This shows a very good plan for all styles of Paletot; the quantity required is double the full length of back. The dotted lines at the bottom, show how in cutting the next garment from the length, the small piece above the sleeve heads may be used up.

Fig. 2.—TOP COAT, on 54-inch cloth. About twice the full length of back will be required; for instance if the length of back from back neck to bottom of skirt is 40½ inches, about 2¼ yards will be wanted.

Fig. 3.—TROWSERS; on a 28-inch material. This is the plan which we think is perhaps the most preferable for general use. No pieces have to be joined in, and the Trowsers look better in consequence. The plumb lines are all exactly parallel to the edge of cloth, so that the Trowsers will hang in the most satisfactory manner. The waistbands can be cut from the outsides of legs, and the piece marked C, will cut the front of a small-sized waistcoat, the piece marked D serving for collar, facings

(Plate 38.)

&c. The length required, is about 3 inches more, than twice the length of Side Seam.

The larger and smaller sizes of Coats, will of course require more or less stuff, and on an average the difference may be estimated as follows: supposing that a coat for a breast measure of 18¾, takes 62 inches of cloth. Then—

A Breast 15¾ will take 50 in. or 12 in. less.
    ,,   17¼   ,,   56 in. or 6 in. less.
    ,,   20¼   ,,   68 in. or 6 in. more.
    ,,   21¾   ,,   74 in. or 12 in. more.

Of course this is merely a very rough estimate or approximation, and is merely intended to serve in some degree as a guide, in ordering the lengths of cloth, and in fixing the price of garments.

With the various lengths and schemes that we have given, a cutter who has a knowledge of arithmetic, can calculate easily by a simple rule-of-three sum, either the difference of the lengths required for larger or smaller sizes, or what lengths would be required, if the mate-

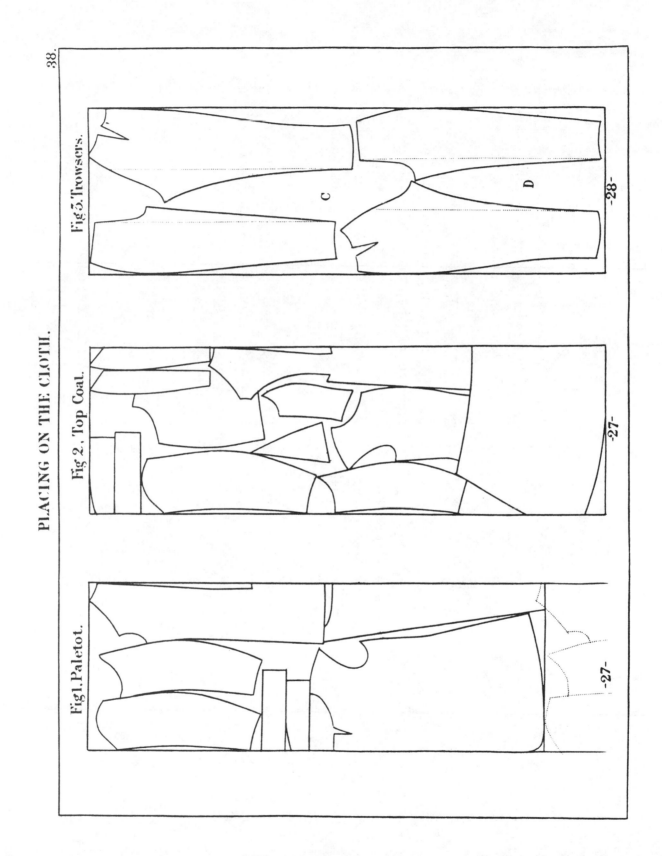

PLACING ON THE CLOTH.

Fig 1. Paletot.   Fig 2, Top Coat.   Fig 3. Trowsers.

-27-   -27-   -28-

C

D

38.

MISFITS.

(*Plate* 39.)

An accurate knowledge of the various kinds of Misfits that may be found, and of the true means of correcting them, is one of the most important acquirements of the scientific cutter.

A cutter using our System has undoubtedly very little occasion for making use of his knowledge of misfits, but some tailors are in the habit of caring very little about the cut of their patterns, and trust to making the pattern fit, by numerous alterations when trying on. This is the principle adopted by all dressmakers, and nothing can be more *unscientific*, or more liable to produce errors. The corrections marked are often quite the opposite to those really required, the garment is subjected to a second series of alterations, and an absolute, irretrievable misfit, is the result.

In some houses, almost every coat requires nearly the same alteration. It may be the armhole which is not forward enough, the shoulder-piece which is too straight, or the forepart

---

(*Plate* 38.)

rial is either wider or narrower than those that we have given.

The quantity of cloth required for Ladies' Riding Habits, will of course vary according to the sizes and the length and fulness of the train. As a rule, if the train is 60 inches long, and 2½ breadths wide, about 5 yards of 54-inch cloth will be required; because the half breadth left will just cut the body and sleeves. If the skirt is not to be so full, or if very wide cloth is used, so that two breadths only are required for the train, then about 4 yards and ⅛ will be wanted: 28 inches of this being for the body.

In cutting out the garments in the cloth, it must be borne in mind that the seams are *not to be allowed for.* All the allowances requisite for the various seams, are given to the pattern by our systems of drafting, without any calculation. Of course layings in may be left if preferred; and the best places for these are:—at the seam under the arm, at the top of shoulder, at the neck seam near the shoulder-point, and at the upper part of scye in the forepart.

(Plate 39.)

which is always too crooked, thus proving that the system by which they cut is radically defective. Some master tailors are so bigoted, and so opposed to all progress or improvement, that they will not allow the use of the graduated measures, and will not have the bust and curve measures taken. Can anyone wonder therefore, that they are punished for their neglect of science, by the great expense they are put to for continual alterations, and by having a coat occasionally thrown on their hands.

The causes of misfits, though apparently very numerous, may by careful examination and comparison, be reduced to a small number of general rules. They may be divided first into two large groups, one consisting of Errors in the Forepart, the other of Errors in the lengths of Back.

On the following plates the plain lines show the defective patterns, the strong black lines the ways of correcting the errors.

FAULTS IN THE FOREPART.

A. *Shoulder-piece too Backward.*

(Plate 39.)

Fig. 1 ; sometimes called Forepart too Crooked. This error in the cut, causes the front edge of forepart to droop or fall away, which is one of the defects most frequently met with. The coat fits well otherwise, but when unbuttoned, the front part is seen to fall away. When buttoned, the crease edge and the neck appear too long. This may sometimes happen even when the cut is perfectly correct, if the workman has stretched the neck in making up, or (which is the same thing) has put on the collar too long.

If the fault is in the cut, the best way is to join a corner on the shoulder-piece, and then cut it straighter and shorter, as shown by A, fig. 1. If the fault arises from the making up, it will be best to take out a fish in the neck seam, as shown by fig. 2, marked A, correction.

B. *Shoulder-piece too Straight.*

Fig. 3.—When the shoulder-point of forepart

MISFITS, FAULTS IN THE FOREPART.

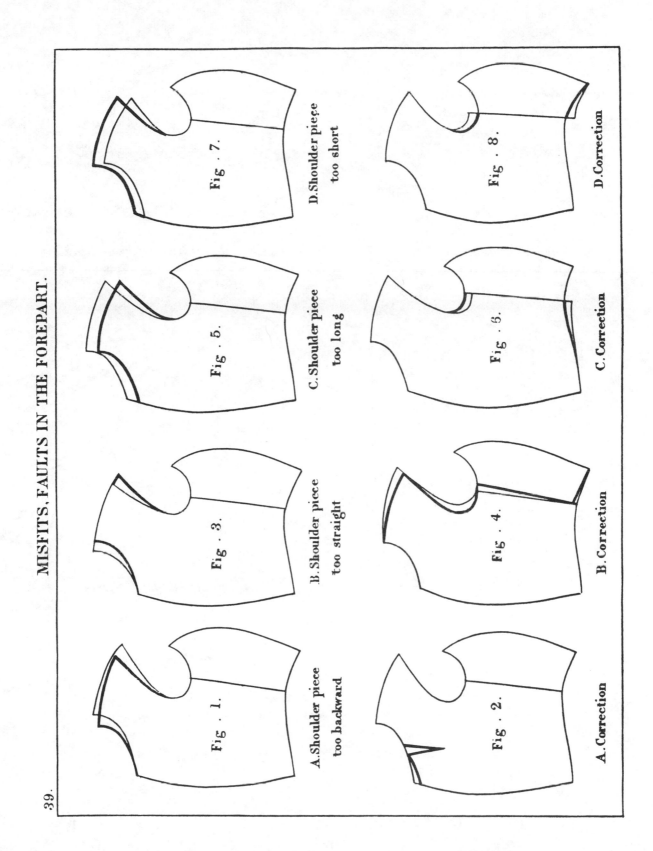

Fig . 1.

A. Shoulder piece too backward

Fig . 2.

A. Correction

Fig . 3.

B. Shoulder piece too straight

Fig . 4.

B. Correction

Fig . 5.

C. Shoulder piece too long

Fig . 6.

C. Correction

Fig . 7.

D. Shoulder piece too short

Fig . 8.

D. Correction

is brought too forward, the coat will crease at the front of scye, which seems to require hollowing out a little ; and the coat will also appear too tight at the neck, and at the back of waist.

The most natural way of correcting this, is of course to take back the shoulder-point, as shown by B, fig. 3 : but this cannot be done unless (which rarely happens) there has been a laying in left at the top of scye. Fig. 4, marked B, correction, shows another plan, which consists in hollowing out the front of scye, and bringing back the diameter of arm to its proper width, by taking out a piece under the arm, gradating to nothing at the hip. This will of course have the effect of narrowing the chest, and if the coat is to be worn buttoned, the buttons must be taken forward to compensate it.

The two misfits that we have just described, will never be found in any pattern drafted by our system, unless it has been carelessly made up. Workmen are very careless about the neck stretching, and to obviate this, we advise all

(*Plate* 39.)

cutters to cut out the collars to the proper length, as explained on *plate 25*, and to tack a piece of stay tape round the neck seam, which is not to be removed until the time for putting on the collar.

All the misfits that we are now about to describe, both in the Forepart and Back, may be termed faults in the balance, and are caused by cutters attempting to draft without the measures of *Bust* and *Curve*. When these measures are not taken, it is a mere chance if the coat has the proper balance, and any error in the balance, however small, produces a corresponding defect in the garment. No amount of care, or of knowledge and experience of structure, can compensate for the chance of error, which arises from neglecting to take the two simple measures called *Bust* and *Curve*.

C. *Shoulder-piece too Long.*

Fig. 5.—This error like fig. 3, causes the front edge to fall away when the coat is worn unbuttoned : besides this, it does not touch at the back part of waist, and forms a long fold

(Plate 39.)

in front of the arm. When buttoned, the coat fits well at the back, but creases all across the chest, on account of the extra length of shoulder-piece.

The most natural way of remedying this fault, is to shorten the shoulder-piece, as shown by fig. 5 ; but this cannot be done if there is no laying in at the top part of the armhole. Again if the garment is finished, this manner of alteration becomes impossible, as the lapel cannot be shortened: the coat therefore, must then be corrected as shown on fig. 6, C, by joining in a piece at the bottom of scye, sewing the side piece higher up, and cutting off the extra length at the bottom of forepart.

D. Shoulder-piece too Short.

Fig. 7.—This error causes the front to draw up, and to be very tight on the chest and round the armhole, and has the same effect, whether the coat is buttoned or not.

If there has been a good laying in left at the neck and top of shoulder, this misfit is easily corrected, as shown by fig. 7. If not,

(Plate 39.)

the correction D, shown on fig. 8, will do equally well. Lower the bottom of scye in the forepart, stitch the side piece lower, and cut off the superfluous length at the bottom of side.

FAULTS IN THE BACK.
E. Back too Long.

(Plate 40.)

Fig. 1.—'This misfit is easily distinguished from all others. The fronts fit perfectly well buttoned or unbuttoned ; but the back forms creases crosswise, between the shoulders and at top, and with the fingers a large fold can be formed across the back, between the shoulders.

The back might be shortened, as shown on E, fig. 1, but as this plan reduces the width of back stretch, it can only be used if the back is too wide as well as too long. The correction E, shown by fig. 2, will have the same result, and is that which is generally the most suitable. Lower the back a little at top : lower the side point, and sew the back lower with the side piece, cutting it across at the

MISFITS. FAULTS IN THE BACK.

40.

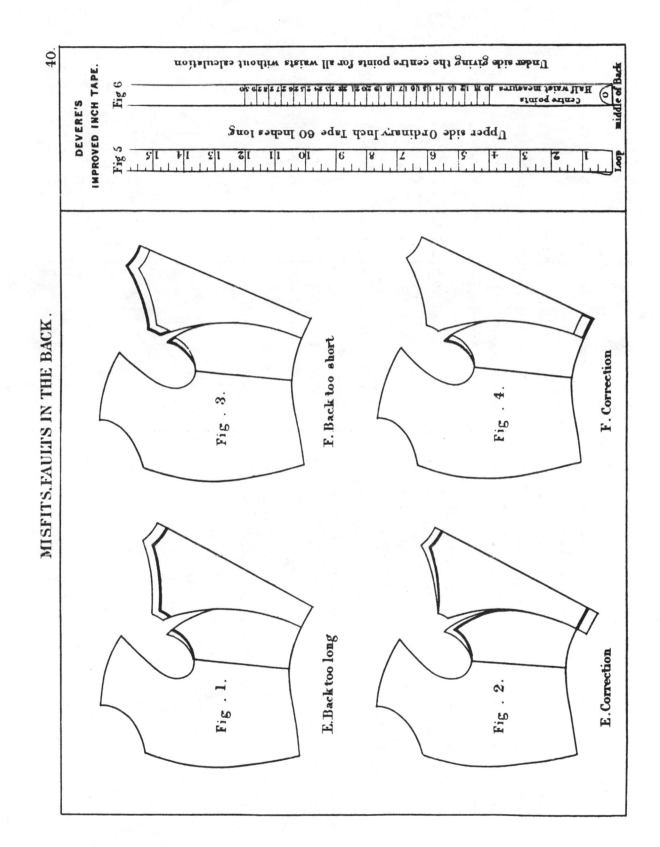

Fig 6
Under side giving the centre points for all waists without calculation

Centre points
middle of Back
Half waist measures 10 11 12 13 14 15 16 17 18 19 20 21 22 23 24 25 26 27 28 29 30

Fig 5
Upper side Ordinary Inch Tape 60 Inches long
1 2 3 4 5 6 7 8 9 10 11 12 13 14 15
Loop

Fig . 3.
F. Back too short

Fig . 4.
F. Correction

Fig . 1.
E. Back too long

Fig . 2.
E. Correction

(Plate 40).

waist, to separate the back skirt, and removing the extra length from the bottom of back.

F. *Back too Short.*

Fig. 3.—When the back is too short, and the coat is unbuttoned, the shortness of the back drags the front edge backward, the bottom of back stands out from the body, and appears as if the coat was immensely too large at this part: it also drags a little at the shoulder, and in front of scye. If the coat is buttoned, it will fit tolerably well at front, but the neck seam is too low behind, the collar stands out from the neck, and the back is instantly seen to be deficient in length.

The proper way of correcting this fault, is of course that shown on fig. 3, but as this can hardly ever be done, the correction indicated by fig. 4 must be made. Join in a piece, so as to raise the side point (or else cut fresh side bodies), and lower the notch at waist, so as to give more length to the back, of course cutting off the bottom of front skirt, to compensate for the necessary shortening of the back skirt.

(Plate 40.)

Summary.

Out of the six kinds of misfits that are to be met with, three of them have the effect of causing the front edge to droop or fall away.

If the forepart is Too Crooked, the drooping of front edge is the only defect to be observed; the coat when buttoned will have no fault but a trifling degree of extra length at neck seam.

If the Shoulder-piece is too long, the front also falls away, but we can distinguish the real cause of the defect, by buttoning the coat, when it forms creases all across the chest, caused by the extra length. Besides this, even when unbuttoned, too long a shoulder-piece causes a long crease in front of the arm, which is not found when the falling away proceeds from other causes.

An unbuttoned coat will also fall away if the Back is too short, but when the coat is buttoned the shortness of back is at once apparent.

The other defects are so very marked, and so very distinct from each other, that there is no occasion for us again to recur to them.

IMPROVED MEASURING-TAPE.
(*Plate* 40.)

From the foregoing remarks our readers will see how important a thing it is to take the measures of *Bust and Curve*, and to apply them in the draft, so as to produce a garment having the proper balance required for each client.

Many students however, find a slight difficulty when taking these measures, to fix the exact place of the CENTRE POINT. We have therefore invented a new kind of Measuring-tape, one side of which contains the ordinary inch measure, and the other gives the exact distance of the CENTRE POINT from the middle of back, for all half waists from 10 to 30 inches, thus avoiding all trouble and calculation when measuring.

Figs. 5 and 6 show sketches of this Improved Tape. It will be seen that the tape has a loop at one end, for taking the measures of Side and Leg seam with great accuracy, as explained on pages 11 and 54.

Further particulars will be found in the advertisement at the end of this work.

SERIES OF PATTERNS.
(*Plate* 41.)

Ready-made Garments now take a very important place in the trade, and a work on Cutting could hardly be considered complete, that did not give some indication of the patterns that are most generally useful for this purpose. At the present time, most tailors always keep a certain number of ready-made garments in stock, which are useful for chance customers, or by a few alterations, will serve for executing very pressing orders, which it would not otherwise be possible to prepare in time.

Of course there are an immense number of different series of patterns for ready-made garments, and we might almost say that each house had its own. A series of patterns suited to one part of Great Britain, may not be found to answer in another : in some districts the stooping pattern will be oftener required than the erect, and in some manufacturing towns, the breast measures will be smaller than for

(*Plate* 41.)

seaports, or for districts in which the population are engaged in active outdoor pursuits.

If we take the average of the whole of Great Britain, we find that out of every hundred garments made—

20	are for Breast measures	between	16 & 17
30	,,	,,	17 & 18
24	,,	,,	18 & $19\frac{1}{4}$
13	,,	,,	$19\frac{1}{4}$ & $20\frac{1}{2}$
8	,,	,,	$20\frac{1}{2}$ & $21\frac{1}{2}$
and 5	are for		$21\frac{3}{4}$ and upwards.

This table may serve as a guide to our readers, in selecting the sizes most likely to be required; of course always bearing in mind the class of customers, and the part of England in which the trade is situated.

On Plate 41, we have given a series of patterns for the Breast measures most often wanted, as shown by the above table: the larger sizes will be less often required than the smaller ones, but we nevertheless give them, because it is in the Stout builds, that the greatest difficulties are met with. Each of

(*Plate* 41.)

these patterns may be drafted by a graduated measure for the size Breast marked on it, or for a size or two larger or smaller. If drafted by the graduated measure marked on it, each pattern will then be for the following measures of the *first series*:—

Fig. 1.—$16\frac{1}{2}$, 15, —$17\frac{3}{4}$, 20, $8\frac{3}{8}$.
Fig. 2.—$17\frac{3}{4}$, $15\frac{1}{4}$,—$18\frac{1}{2}$, $20\frac{7}{8}$, $8\frac{1}{2}$.
Fig. 3.—$19\frac{3}{4}$, $19\frac{1}{4}$,—$19\frac{1}{4}$, $21\frac{7}{8}$, $8\frac{3}{8}$.
Fig. 4.—21, $22\frac{5}{8}$,—$19\frac{3}{4}$, $22\frac{1}{2}$, $8\frac{3}{8}$.

We have omitted the $18\frac{3}{4}$ Breast or proportionate pattern from this series, because it has already been given in Plate 3. We may observe however, that in using the proportionate pattern for ready-made stock, it is as well to allow a little extra width at waist, as slightly stout waists are now more often met with than proportionate or thin ones, and besides this nearly all garments are now required to be easy fitting.

These patterns also show the gradual development of the Human Body, from youth to middle age. Fig. 1 is for a youth, Long Bodied

(Plate 41.)

and proportionately rather thick at Waist, because the chest is not developed. Fig. 2 is still slightly Long Bodied, but the chest has begun to develope, while the waist has hardly increased from fig. 2. In the PROPORTIONATE pattern (see *plate 3*), the man has arrived at his full growth: the chest is large, and the waist comparatively smaller than in fig. 1 or 2, and all the parts of the body have an exact proportion or harmony between each other.

In fig. 3, we see quite a different development: the lengths have hardly increased at all; the Breast measure has increased, but in a much less degree than the Waist, which has now become almost equal to the breast: the structure is Short Bodied and Stout. On fig. 4 the same process goes on, the lengths show hardly any increase; the Breast has increased a little, and the Waist a good deal, so that the structure is become Short Bodied and Very Stout at Waist. After a few years more, he will become still Stouter at Waist, and Shorter

(Plate 41.)

Bodied, and will require the pattern given in Part 1, *plate* 11, figs. 3 and 4.

If the client retains his health, this process of increase will go on still further, until at last it is stopped by the hand of time.

A man who enjoys good health, and lives in accordance with the laws of nature, will go through all the stages of development that we have just described, and which Shakespeare, centuries ago, so accurately delineated in his "Seven Ages."

STOUT WAISTED STRUCTURES.

We will here add a few remarks, on the pattern for very Stout Men, fig. 4, *plate* 41, and 3 & 4, *plate* 11, and will indicate a slight alteration which should be made in drafting for these builds. The *Bust, Curve,* and *Side* measures, are used in the draft in the usual way : the waist is ruled as usual by taking the middle of waist at $6\frac{1}{2}$ as a starting point, and giving half the measure to the front, and half at the back, less the width of back at waist. The

STANDARD PATTERNS FOR VARIOUS SIZES.

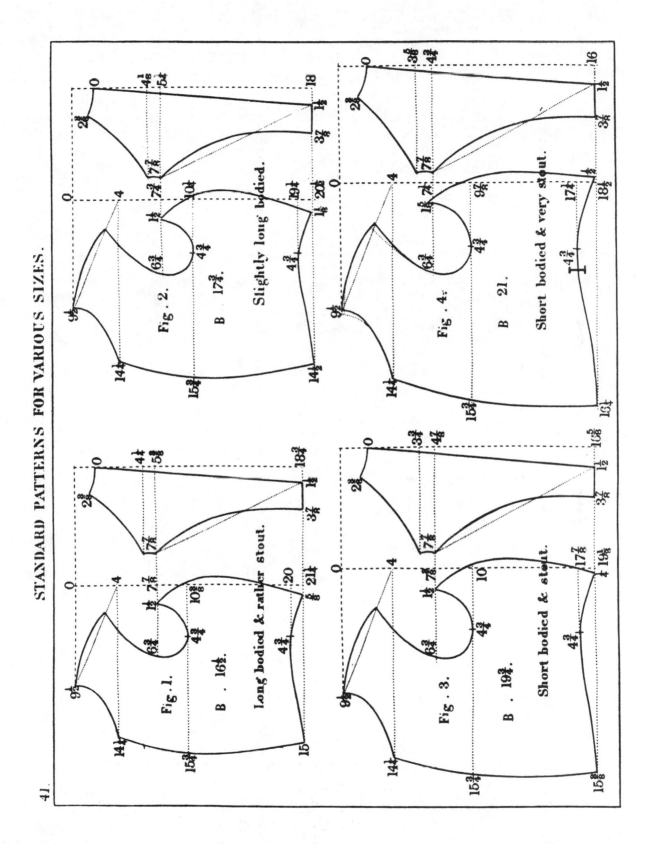

Fig. 1.

B. 16½.

Long bodied & rather stout.

Fig. 2.

B. 17¾.

Slightly long bodied.

Fig. 3.

B. 19¾.

Short bodied & stout.

Fig. 4.

B. 21.

Short bodied & very stout.

41.

(Plate 41.)

difference to make for Very Stout men is, that the side point must be cut a little higher, and must be a little advanced, say to $1\frac{3}{4}$, or even 2 for extreme sizes; the front of scye must remain at its usual place, without any change.

The effect of this change in the place of side point, is to allow a little extra width at the bottom of seam under the arm, which is required on account of the deposit of fat at this part. This change is made on precisely the same principles as those already explained for Paletots, when we raise up and advance the side point, to allow for the fish under the arm; only for stout men, this fish is not taken out, because extra stuff is wanted at the hip, to cover the increase of size at that part. In other words; for Very Stout men, the increase of waist, as compared with the proportionate structure, is provided for as follows:—Half the increase is given at the bottom of front edge; about one-sixth, or a little more, at the bottom of the seam under the arm; and the remainder to the bottom of side body.

(Plate 41.)

Some stout men again, are found to have the stomach very prominent, and the back very hollow, and for these the shoulder-point may be a little advanced, say to about 10 or $10\frac{1}{4}$. This will have exactly the same effect, as if the fore-part had a piece taken in at the bottom of side, and added on to the front of waist; thus providing for the variation required for this build, without making any alteration in the draft.

DRAFT TO MEASURE
WITH
THE COMMON INCH TAPE ONLY.

(Plate 42.)

In the draft of all the garments that we have described in this work, the *fixed points* (that is—those points that are not altered by variations in structure), are always marked by a graduated measure, corresponding to the Breast measure of the client, and this manner of drafting is the simplest and surest of all; it avoids the necessity for tedious and often complicated calculations, and all risk of making errors is avoided.

(Plate 42.)

There are, however, many persons who object to the use of graduated measures, and prefer to mark all the fixed points of a pattern, by divisions or fractions of the Breast measure, notwithstanding the extra trouble and loss of time they entail upon themselves by this prejudice. Some of these are under the delusion, that the working of our system is entirely dependent upon the graduated measures : this is however not the case ; our system can be worked just as well *without the graduated measures, as with them,* and with equally good results. The only disadvantage is that the pattern will take somewhat longer to draft, because of the time occupied in making the proper calculations for the various divisions of the breast.

Some twenty years ago, the use of the graduated measures was a thing almost unknown to English cutters. Since that time they have gradually been coming into more general use, and in a few years more, we expect that no tailor will think of drafting without graduated measures, any more than he would of cutting

(Plate 42.)

out his cloth with a penknife, instead of with his shears. Graduated scales are used in most professions, and in all mechanical arts. An architect or civil engineer, who attempted to make his drawings by calculating fractional divisions of the original dimensions of his plan, would be laughed at by the whole of his brethren. All designers for manufactures employ graduated scales, and where they are not used in any department, it is a sign that that branch of art is in a very primitive stage, and that they are only working by the rule of thumb.

The diagrams on *plate 42,* give a Coat, Waistcoat, and Paletot, having letters placed at all the principal points, and we will now proceed to explain how these garments may be drafted by the common inch tape only:—using the Measures explained in Part I, to mark all the principal points, and ruling the dimensions of other parts of the pattern by divisions of the Breast measure.

This manner of drafting may be often found serviceable, if as sometimes happens, the gra-

(*Plate 42.*)

duated measures are mislaid or destroyed, or if the cutter is in an establishment where the use of graduated measures is objected to.

COATS. FIG. 1.

Measures used : Breast, Waist, Curve, Bust, Side.

Formation of the Squares.

A B,—About one-fourth more than the *Breast* measure. A C,—One-third of A B. Draw the outside lines of square and the construction line of forepart.

Back.

A D,—The Balance or difference between the *Bust* and *Curve* Measures.

D E,—Length of back ; ruled at 1½ less than the *Curve* measure.

D F,—¾ of an inch more than a fourth of D E. Draw lines square across at F and E, the line at F, crossing the construction line of forepart at G, and giving the height of side point ; and the line from E, touching the construction line of forepart at S.

D H,—One-eighth of the Breast.

(*Plate 42.*)

E I,—One-twelfth.

I J,—Width of bottom of back to Fashion.

G K,—One-sixteenth of the Breast.

Forepart.

C L,—⅛ of an inch more than half the Breast.

C M, and B N, each half A C.

N O, and G Q,—Each one-twelfth the Breast.

Draw a line from L to M, and make L P the same length as H K.

Q R,—About ½ an inch more than a fourth.

S T,—One-fourth.

S U,—¼ of an inch more than one-third of the Breast.

T V, and U W,—Each one-sixteenth.

V X,—Length of *Side* to measure.

W Y,—Half the waist measure.

W Z,—Half the waist measure less the width of back at waist.

Draw all the curves as explained in Part 1, *plate* 3.

If the supplementary series of measures has been taken, the pattern may now be corrected by them, as shown by fig. 1, *plate* 6.　The

(Plate 42.)

waist must be lengthened according to Fashion or to measure, and the collar, lapel, skirt, &c. added, according to the style required.

WAISTCOATS. FIGS. 2 & 3.

Measures used: Breast, Waist, Curve, Bust, Side.

For this garment, the back and forepart are drafted separately, commencing with

The Back, Fig. 3.

A B,—Length of *Curve* to measure.
B C,—Length of *Side* to measure.
A D,—One-sixth of the Breast.
Draw lines square across at B, C, and D.
A E,—One-eighth.
D F,—Three times A E.
C G, $1\frac{1}{4}$ more than half the Breast.
B H,—$1\frac{1}{2}$ more than half the Waist measure.

The Forepart, Fig. 2.

A B,—Length of *Bust* to measure.
B C,—One-eighth of the Breast.
C D,—Length of *Side* to measure.
A E,—$\frac{3}{8}$ of an inch less than one-eighth.
A F,—One-fourth of the Breast.

(Plate 42.)

F G,—Half F D.
Draw square lines at F, G, D, C, and B.
A H,—1 inch more than a fourth.
D I,—$1\frac{1}{4}$ more than half.
F J,—$\frac{5}{8}$ of an inch less than D I.
G K,—$\frac{3}{8}$ of an inch more than one-eighth.
C L,—One-twelfth.
L M,—Half the Waist measure.

The curves of back and forepart are drawn as shown by figs. 3 and 4 of *plate* 13, and the waistcoat is made of the particular style required, as shown on *plates* 15 and 16.

PALETOTS. FIG. 4.

Measures required: Breast, Waist, Curve, Bust, Side, and Full Length.

The back and forepart, as for coats, are drafted side by side in two squares.

Formation of the Squares.

A B,—$1\frac{5}{8}$ inch more than half the Breast.
B C, $\frac{5}{8}$ of an inch more than five-sixths of the Breast.

Draw the outside lines of square, and the construction line of forepart B g.

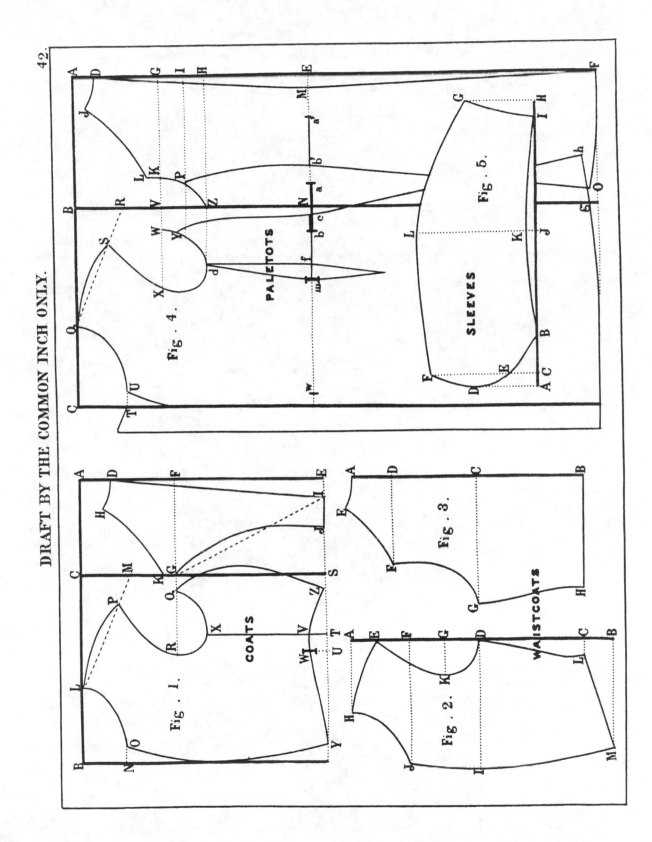

DRAFT BY THE COMMON INCH ONLY.

COATS. Fig. 1.

WAISTCOATS. Fig. 2. Fig. 3.

PALETOTS. Fig. 4.

SLEEVES. Fig. 5.

42.

(Plate 42.)

The Back.

A D,—$\frac{3}{4}$ of an inch less than the Balance, or difference between *Bust* and *Curve* measures.

D E,—1$\frac{1}{2}$ inch less than the *Curve* measure.

D F,—Full Length to measure.

E H,—Length of *Side* to measure.

G I,—The extra depth given to the back scye, according to Fashion or to taste.

Draw lines square across at all these points. The line at G gives the front of scye. The line at I serves to rule the height of side point in the forepart. The line at H crosses the construction line at Z, and also gives the depth of the bottom of scye in the forepart. The line at E, is the waist line, and crosses the construction line of forepart at N. The line at F shows the full lengths both of forepart and back.

D J,—About $\frac{2}{8}$ of an inch more than one-eighth of the Breast.

G K,—About 1$\frac{1}{8}$ of an inch less than half.

K L,—One-sixteenth.

Draw a regular curve from L to Z, crossing

(Plate 42.)

the line from I at point P, which gives the correct form of the back scye.

E M,—One-twelfth or less.

M b',—Width of back to Fashion or to taste.

E a',—half G K.

F O,—Width of bottom, about 3 or 4 more than M b'.

The Forepart.

B Q,—$\frac{1}{8}$ of an inch more than half the breast.

B R, and C T,—Each a little less than half G K of the back.

Q S,—Same length as J L of the back.

T U,—One-twelfth.

V W,—$\frac{1}{4}$ of an inch more than one-twelfth.

W X,—$\frac{1}{4}$ of an inch more than a fourth.

Y is the side point, marked a little higher than the point where the square line from I crosses the curved line drawn from W to d.

Z d,—One-fourth.

N m,—$\frac{1}{4}$ of an inch more than a third the breast.

(Plate 42.)

m w,—1 inch more than half the waist.

m a,—Half the waist.

a b,—The same as the distance between a' b' of the back.

b c,—Any extra fulness, according to taste.

m f,—Fish under the arm, more or less according to the fulness required; never more than one-twelfth.

g h, about one-fourth or more, according to the fulness required.

The lapel is drawn to Fashion or taste, and all the curves are drawn by the hand as explained in *plate 28*.

SLEEVES. FIG. 5.

A B,—$\frac{3}{8}$ of an inch less than a fourth.

A C,—One-sixteenth.

A D,—$\frac{1}{4}$ of an inch more than one-fourth.

C E,—One-eighth or rather less.

C F,—$\frac{3}{4}$ of an inch less than half for Coats; only $\frac{3}{8}$ of an inch less for Overcoats.

F G,—Full Length to measure, deducting the back stretch.

(Plate 42.)

G H,—Wrist, to measure or to Fashion.

H I,—One-twelfth.

I J,—Half I B.

J K,—Curve of forearm seam to Fashion.

K L,—Elbow width, to Fashion or to taste. The curves are drawn as usual.

———

By the aid of these diagrams, the student may now by a little ingenuity, apply the draft by the common inch, to Topcoats, Loose Paletots, and indeed to all styles of garments. We have already given in Part 2, the way of drafting TROWSERS without the use of graduated measures.

We must again repeat, however, that a cutter, whether by our system or any other, is losing his time, giving himself much unnecessary labour, and running great risk of error, by neglecting to use the graduated measures, unless in a case of absolute necessity, such as the loss of the graduated measures, or any other similar accident, which cannot very often occur.

SELECTION OF STOCK,

OR THE PURCHASE OF MATERIALS.

In buying your stock, you should always avoid what you can do without. To keep the stock within proper limits, though difficult, is very important; but by keeping rigidly to the rule of buying only those articles that are absolutely essential for your particular trade and class of customers, and by selecting materials, colours, and styles, that you know by experience will be approved of, you cannot go far wrong.

For the Winter trade, the overcoat is of course the most important study, and as a rule, likely to be the safest things you can buy. soft warm materials, such as the Elysian, Witney, or Pilot. or any similar class of goods, are Some good trades never keep anything else for *stock*, and have a good number of patterns to show their customers for novelties: this is a safe rule to adhere to, unless you have a good chance trade in a leading thoroughfare.

For a chance trade, the newest colours and styles for the window are the best, and for Winter always buy a few of the newest waistcoats you can get, and show them early, before your customers can see them elsewhere.

Be careful in buying Winter Trowserings, and bear in mind that cold weather is sure to come early or late; therefore select good, heavy, neat, useful, styles. Scotch Angolas are very appropriate, and Platt's Winter Tweeds are heavy, durable, and warm.

In Trowserings, always keep good, medium, proved, articles; not so common as to be likely to get you into trouble, through not wearing well, nor so dear that your customers leave on account of the prices.

Spring is the time to buy, in anticipation of a good trade in trowserings: as a rule there are three or four pairs sold in Summer, for one in Winter. Always buy a few of the newest things you can get;—short lengths, unless the article seems likely to be in great demand.

Oxford and mixed Meltons of good quality, are always in demand for Spring and Summer

Walking-coats, and so are black and blue fine cloths for Frockcoats. It is a good plan to keep a few short lengths of the greatest novelties in fancy Coatings, and in Tweeds, &c. for Tourists' Suits. Keep a good stock of white and light-coloured Waistcoats: if kept ready-made they are always useful and sell freely.

Always keep a fair assortment of light water-proof Tweed Overcoats ready made, so that they are always at hand, to introduce to customers on rainy days, or for the Races, &c., &c. It is these little incidental things, that increase your trade above the average, and keep your customers from going to the ready-made houses.

One or two pieces of black Cloth and Doe-skin, should always be kept in stock ready for use.

A good supply of trimmings should always be kept; these things are bought much cheaper wholesale than retail, when seen about the place they look as though business were being done, and when wanted, it saves a great deal of time and trouble, if they are ready at hand. Always buy *early in the season*; stocks left on hand have generally been bought too late, when the rush of trade is falling off. Make it a rule to show your goods early, and so get the name of having the newest things. Besides this, an article attracts from its freshness to the eye, and if you show it after every one else, the effect is much less in your favour.

A FEW HINTS

TO THOSE ABOUT TO COMMENCE BUSINESS.

We will now suggest a few things to a young tradesman, just thinking of starting in business for himself.

Firstly—Not to do so, unless he has some money; and if he has, to take a house, in some good thoroughfare if possible, but at any rate in the best situation that his means or connection will justify him in taking.

Secondly.—Having taken his house, he should select some good draper; state to him fairly and openly, his capital and prospects of success, and ask him for the most favourable terms of credit he can give. Keep to one or two houses at starting, not more. Whatever the terms are, *be sure and pay to time.*

Then watch carefully the draper's prices ; if goods can be obtained cheaper elsewhere, tell him so, and give him the option of still serving you at the prices you can buy of others. If he declines, state the case to the other party, show invoices and receipts, to prove the arrangement made and how it has been kept. This will engender confidence, and the life-blood of success, *good credit*, will be obtained, and will in some degree supply the place of capital.

A man is sure to buy well, who always pays in time : all drapers are too much afraid of losing so valuable a customer. Tailors as a rule, are very indifferent as to paying in time (even when they have the money), and they little think how dearly they pay for their neglect.

In selecting goods, buy for yourself : never be influenced by the representations of travellers and others : remember they live by selling. There are indeed, men to be met with who study their customers' interest, and only recommend those goods that are safe to buy : if you meet with such a draper, prize him at his proper value : they are rare.

Avoid another great mistake made by many : calculate beforehand, the lengths you mean to have. As trade progresses, a small income may be saved by carefully studying the proper lengths to have, and by always paying to time so that the trade are always willing and ready to serve you at the minimum of rate of profit. Always avoid overbuying. Woollen goods are like horses, a continual running expense, as interest must be added for keeping and deterioration. Still do not rush to the opposite extreme. We have known many good trades quite spoilt, through starving the stock.

No matter how your personal expenses may suffer, always try to avoid that first step into difficulties and debt, which if it lead not to bankruptcy, at any rate takes away for a time a man's independence, by placing him in the hands of his creditors.

Remember as a master, you must be more than a mere foreman. Learn enough book-keeping to know how to manage your own affairs, and be enough of the tradesman to know how to buy, how to sell, and how to see that those about you are doing their duty, and keeping stock, &c. in proper order. Do not be compelled to have your young men or your cutter at your elbow, to ask their advice on everything: think and act for yourself; if you cannot buy properly on your own judgment, you ought not to be in business.

Have the time of credit understood: send in your accounts when due, and if your customer does not pay in a reasonable time, have no more to do with him. Serve your customers well, so that you need fear no competition. *Sell nothing you are ashamed of*, in the end it would get you into trouble.

Watch your ledger at stated intervals, and periodically remind those customers who have not paid to time. Keep a diary, and enter all engagements. *Always be punctual*, no matter how insignificant the transaction: in fact, act in all things so as to obtain the good opinion of others, and to retain your own self-respect. Proper system and determination, will render unnecessary the chicanery so prevalent at the present time.

You must not forget the item of " Profit Discount." If the prices are the same, those houses, which allow five per cent. for cash, and send all parcels free, must be the cheapest. We will suggest for the basis of your own system of credit: to allow five per cent. to your customer for payment within a month of delivery; 2½ per cent. if paid in three months, and *nett* at six months.

Give the greatest possible attention to the cut of all garments, and spare no trouble to render the fit as perfect as possible, and to have all the details of the cut and making up, in accordance with the latest fashion. Have a special pattern cut to suit each client, and do not trust to alterations made when trying on; they are troublesome to the customer, and give him a very mean idea of your talent; they are an expense to the master, a trouble to the workman, and rarely produce a good result. Bear in mind that the principles of cutting elucidated in this work, cannot be far deviated from, without great risk of error, and that no amount of care in other departments of business, can compensate the customers for the annoyance and dissatisfaction caused by a faulty System of Cutting, or a defective fit.

Stamp your trade from the commencement with some leading article, something that everyone will want; make it well, let the material be always good, and charge it low, so that you can introduce it to everyone with confidence, as an article not be beaten elsewhere.

The first thing is to become known, the next and most important is to gain your customer's confidence.

Get known in your own neighbourhood; circulars or handbills and local advertisements are often advantageous, and these, combined with selling some one article better and cheaper than anyone else, and with care in buying, punctuality in paying, skill and success in cutting, honesty in dealing, and tact in managing, are sure eventually to gain sufficient support to make your position a firm and lasting one, and in the end to secure an independence.

RECEIPT FOR WATERPROOFING.

We here give a receipt for making every kind of woollen, cotton, or linen material waterproof, and it will be found, if practised, of immense value and advantage to the trade :—

Take one ounce of alum, and dissolve it in a quart of water : in another vessel dissolve one ounce of acetate or sugar of lead, also in a quart of water : when the alum and lead are entirely dissolved, empty one vessel into that which contains the other : mix them well together by stirring them with a stick, then leave it for a time to settle, and when a deposit is formed at the bottom, pour the liquid gently off into another vessel, leaving the waste deposit behind. The liquid part being now ready, immerse the material to be rendered waterproof, leaving it a little time to soak, then press it with the hands to get some of the water out, and hang it on a line to dry.

This manner of rendering materials waterproof, does not alter either the colour or the pliability of the material: it also allows the escape of the perspiration.

There will be a faint smell at first, something like vinegar, but it will go off in about two days.

To prove the efficacy of the recipe, try first on a small piece of cloth or alpaca; you will find that you may carry water about in it, without a single drop passing through.

The quantities given above will be sufficient to waterproof a Paletot or coat: should larger quantities be required, use a quart of water to each ounce of alum and a quart to each ounce of sugar of lead. We must remind our readers that very coarse stout cloths are not suited for this operation, which is most successful when applied to finer materials, such as Tweeds, &c., &c., which it will render sufficiently waterproof to protect the wearer against the effects of an ordinary shower, though indeed, unless the cloth was very fine, and the waterproofing very well done, it might not be proof against a whole day's heavy rain.

CONCLUDING REMARKS.

DURING the progress of this HANDBOOK through the press, we have been induced to extend it considerably beyond the limits we had at first assigned for the work, and instead of short abridged sketches, we have given full and detailed descriptions of everything connected with the Profession. This work therefore combined with "THE TAILOR'S GUIDE," will be found to contain all the information necessary for a thorough knowledge of the Tailor's Art.

"THE TAILOR'S GUIDE" most fully classifies and delineates all the various structures, and shows the particular form and cut which must be given to a pattern, to suit each of these builds: the general and theoretical knowledge contained in that work, is applicable alike to all systems of Cutting.

The present HANDBOOK carries into daily practice all the knowledge contained in the "GUIDE." It shows the best and simplest system of Measurement, and the easiest and quickest, as well as the most certain and accurate manner, of drafting all garments, so as to produce in the draft, by the direct application of the measures themselves, all the variations of form required to suit each structure.

The marked success which has attended the present work, and the numerous and flattering testimonials that we have received, show that this portion of our labors, has given the greatest satisfaction to our patrons, throughout the British Empire.

GENERAL INDEX.